HOW TO CF
A SUCCESSFUL
MUSIC ENSEMBLE

RUNNING YOUR GROUP &
ARRANGING THE MUSIC

PATRICK GAZARD

R· RHINEGOLD
EDUCATION

First published 2012 in Great Britain by
Rhinegold Education
14–15 Berners Street
London W1T 3LJ, UK

www.musicroom.com

© 2012 Rhinegold Education
a division of Music Sales Limited

HOW TO CREATE A SUCCESSFUL MUSIC ENSEMBLE
Order No. RHG403
ISBN: 978-1-78038-246-3

Exclusive Distributors:
Music Sales Ltd
Distribution Centre, Newmarket Road
Bury St Edmunds, Suffolk IP33 3YB, UK

Printed in the EU

**Book companion website: www.hybridpublications.com
Access code: FJ643**

DEDICATION

This book is dedicated to all the musicians past and present who I have had the pleasure of directing. Remember: just because I didn't do it when you were there does not mean it is not a good idea now!

'Amateurs should be professional in attitude, and professionals should be amateur in spirit'

(Geoffrey Stark, father of Peter Stark
of the Ernest Read Symphony Orchestra)

LCHORALSTYLESARRANGING
ANNINGVENUEVOCALSDYNAMICS
ONDUCTINGADMINISTRATION
VENUESOUNDDYNAMICSMANAGING
PTEACHINGCONDUCTINGLIGHTING
ORMANCEPRACTICALITIES
TINGSCORINGTEACHINGVENUE
ENUEDYNAMICSMANAGINGCHORAL
RCUSSIONINSTRUMENTAL
LIGHTINGSCORINGSTYLES

ABOUT THE AUTHOR

Patrick Gazard has almost 25 years' experience in music and music education, during which he has run numerous youth and adult ensembles, both instrumental and choral. Now a freelance musician, Patrick has had arrangements published by Music Sales, Banks Music Publications and Faber Music. He currently directs three ensembles – two Big Bands and the Stage Choir – at the High Wycombe Music Centre, (and reached the National Finals of Music for Youth in 2011 and 2012 with different groups). He is also the founder and Musical Director of the Marlow Youth Chamber Orchestra workshops. Patrick is the author of *You Can Teach Primary Music*, also published by Rhinegold Education.

www.patrickgazard.co.uk

ACKNOWLEDGEMENTS

I have been fortunate to be assisted by numerous musical experts, most notably those who have given their time to provide case studies of their various ensembles: John Davie, Gillian Dibden, David Hill and Peter Stark.

Thanks also to members of the Cobweb Orchestra (Catherine Shackell), the Roade Community Orchestra from Northamptonshire (Tim Chisholm/Ian Ridley), and The Elmbridge Community Big Band (Cliff Van Tonder/Georgi Bartlett). In particular I would like to credit Paul Eshelby, current director of the National Youth Jazz Orchestra's Second band (NYJO 2). As leader of the Big Band Summer School at the Benslow Music Trust, not only did he encourage me as a young arranger but he also taught me a great deal about rehearsal technique and repertoire choice.

I am also indebted to top West End arranger David Cullen for his advice and support.

And lastly to all the various conductors and musical directors from whom I have unashamedly stolen ideas and techniques over the years: I could not have done it without you.

ALCHORALSTYLESARRANGING
PLANNINGVENUEVOCALSDYNAMICS
SCONDUCTINGADMINISTRATION
YVENUESOUNDDYNAMICSMANAGING
UPTEACHINGCONDUCTINGLIGHTING
RFORMANCEPRACTICALITIES
CTINGSCORINGTEACHINGVENUE
YVENUEDYNAMICSMANA
PERCUSSIONINSTRUMENTAL
PLIGHTINGSCORINGSTYLES

GUIDE TO THE
ONLINE RESOURCES

BOOK COMPANION WEBSITE

The following supplementary material to support the book is available on the book's companion website:

www.hybridpublications.com

Access code: FJ643

Chapters 1 and 6
- Further auditioning and rehearsal tips

Chapter 3
- Basic conducting techniques

Chapter 8
- Copyright and licensing Q&A

Chapter 9
- Interview with *Strictly Come Dancing* arranger: Dave Arch
- Interview with pop/disco arranger: Richard Niles
- List of arrangers and orchestrators
- Examples of introduction and ending techniques/approaches
- Modulation via a suspended note

Chapter 10
- Descants, countermelodies and modulation
- Choral arranging: additional part-writing examples
- SATB and piano arrangement of 'I Gave my Love a Cherry'

Chapter 11
- 'Daisy Bell' variations – score and audio examples of 'starts' in each of the models discussed
- 'Daisy Bell' full arrangement

Also available
- Useful website links
- Patrick Gazard's ensemble directing experience

I remember what got me hooked on what's turned out to be a lifetime's journey of music making. No, it wasn't the hours practising scales, improving technique, preparing for solo performances and exams! No matter how good (mostly), and satisfying (almost always) these experiences were, nothing compared to the buzz of being in ensembles – always about the music, but so much more.

It's been an absolute joy, therefore, to have spent over a decade at Youth Music helping a generation of youngsters get into and immerse themselves in this wonderful world of group music making. Meanwhile, the number of adults looking for similar stimulating high quality opportunities has been on the rise too.

However, this increasing appetite amongst all ages to participate is now matched by a real need for more skilled musicians willing and able to create, lead, direct, and facilitate these amateur music ensembles. If you're one such musician already doing it – bravo! If it's virgin territory, or you've thought about it but never made the first move – step forward please, hesitate no longer!

Drawing on years of experience – his own and others' – Patrick Gazard offers here a really practical guide to creating, running and arranging for amateur music ensembles. For musicians already experienced in running ensembles, there's likely to be much reaffirmation, but also ideas for refreshment. If you're less experienced or a novice, it offers a particular way in – a launch-pad – and possible life-saver. It's also helpfully set out so you can dip into it for what you need, when you need it.

Listening to ensembles – instrumental, vocal, mixed, covering a range of styles and cultural traditions – up and down the country, reminds me that each has its own distinctive dynamic. Gazard helps to unpack so many of the elements involved in creating that dynamic, with handy tips, techniques and practical examples in abundance. It's a helpful reminder too, that although performance is the end product for most ensembles, what brings the group to life is every-thing that's happened before the 'big day'. Rehearsals, repertoire choice, how the group is led and facilitated, and so on, keeps the group energised, eager to carry on to the next challenge and the buzz of creating more thrilling music together.

There are few other ways in which people – often total strangers – from very diverse backgrounds and varying levels of musical ability, devote hours of their time regularly, voluntarily, to create their ensemble, their musical community. Woven into the musical life, there's friendship, companionship, and more – emotional release and stress-busting just two. 'Amateur', denoting the love and commitment they bring to it, also often belies the high levels of professionalism and musical standards aimed for and achieved.

To be the catalyst creating the group dynamic, releasing all sorts of passions and helping people to create good music together is amazing and enormously rewarding. There are few other fields of endeavour quite like it. I hope this guide is useful for you. Read – and enjoy.

Christina Coker OBE
Chief Executive, Youth Music

Christina has led Youth Music (National Foundation for Youth Music) since its inception in 1999. Committed to helping children and young people with least opportunity discover their creativity and potential through music making, over 2.5 million have benefited to date.

'It is a truth universally acknowledged, that a singer in possession of extensive choral experience must be in want of a choir.'

(With apologies to Jane Austen)

Frequently challenging, often intimidating and sometimes unappreciated, but ultimately rewarding and creatively fulfilling, the role of an ensemble leader is not an easy one. This book is designed to support you with the practicalities of running a group and making it successful, whether you are a solo musician taking the reins or a schoolteacher tasked with running the extra-curricular musical life of the school. It is likely you won't have much experience of running rehearsals, selecting repertoire or preparing for concerts, and even more likely that you will have to learn on the job, but your desire to inspire your musicians and the thrill of that ultimate performance will make it all worthwhile.

WHO IS THIS BOOK FOR?

This book is predominantly aimed at those individual musicians who have yet to experience the thrill of running a music ensemble or who would like to learn more about it. The reader may be a teacher of individuals or in a school; or may be well known as a successful musician in the local community. Whatever their situation, they will all have one thing in common: the desire to run a musical group and to make it as successful as possible.

WHAT CONSTITUTES AN ENSEMBLE?

For the purposes of this book a musical ensemble is defined as one consisting of ten or more members. Small groups in any genre – string quartet, brass quintet, rock band, jazz quintet – are unlikely to need a separate director, as any leadership will almost certainly be done from inside the group. However, members of such groups may still find the 'Arranging' section useful, especially if they are considering the possibility of combining with other players. There are many ensembles that fall outside the scope of this book, although it is hoped that any directors of such ensembles might still find something of value here.

HOW TO USE THIS BOOK

Depending on the reader's ensemble experience, this book can be dipped in and out of at will. An experienced group leader might go straight to 'Part IV: Arranging for your ensemble' to add a new skill to their armoury, whereas another ensemble director might turn to 'Part III: Rehearsing and performing' for tips and advice on improving rehearsal efficiency, and an absolute beginner might read from cover to cover before embarking on their project.

At various places throughout the text the author pre-empts questions from the reader and introduces an imaginary voice to raise key points. Hopefully the reader will find their concerns addressed in a practical way.

Case studies

Throughout the text there are several case studies detailing how real directors and administrators have gone about forming and maintaining their own musical ensembles over a period of time. There is a wide range here, and it is hoped that the reader will find their experiences and advice useful.

Musical arranging

A unique aspect of this book is the section on arranging for the ensemble. This is detailed and practical, and is predominantly aimed at the ensemble director, although there is no reason why the guidance should not be just as useful for any amateur arranger who might be another member of the group or even an outsider. However, it is clearly not an absolute necessity for you to arrange for your group, and plenty of advice is given on choosing existing repertoire.

Arranging examples

Throughout Part IV there are references to specific songs or pieces to illustrate the various points. Readers should feel free to substitute their own examples where appropriate, as the author can only draw from his experience and there may be more relevant or suitable pieces to support the guidance given.

The author has devised recordings of the musical examples to help illustrate the points made in Chapters 9, 10 and 11. These are available on the book's companion website. The final two specific arrangement approaches merely give a flavour of the possibilities open to the arranger and are not intended to be definitive. Complete versions of both of these arrangements by the author are also available to download from the book's companion website (www.hybridpublications.com, access code: FJ643).

It is assumed that the reader is musically able, reasonably experienced in performing and can read staff notation. A decent grasp of basic harmony will be an advantage, although not a necessity.

NTALCHORALSTYLESARRANGING
GPLANNINGVENUEVOCALSDYNAMICS
NGCONDUCTINGADMINISTRATION
ITYVENUESOUNDDYNAMICSMANAGING
T-UPTEACHINGCONDUCTINGLIGHTING
ERFORMANCEPRACTICALITIES
DUCTINGSCORINGTEACHINGVENUE
TYVENUEDYNAMICSMANAGINGCHORAL
NPERCUSSIONINSTRUMENTAL
HIPLIGHTINGSCORINGSTYLES
BERSHOPPERFORMANCESTART-UP
ITYVENUEINSTRUMENTALVOCALS
MINISTRATIONDYNAMICSCHORAL
PERCUSSIONMODULATIONSOUND
RALSTYLESPERFORMANCEVENUE
TYVENUESTYLESLIGHTINGSCORING
DDYNAMICSMANAGINGCONDUCTING
GMODULATIONWRITINGPERCUSSION
NINGLIGHTINGSCORINGSOUND
VENUECHORALPERFORMANCE
USSIONMODULATIONSOUNDDYNAMICS
ATIONPUBLICITYVENUELIGHTING
CHINGCONDUCTINGMODULATION
PUBLICITYVENUEPERCUSSION
INGADMINISTRATIONPUBLICITY
SHOPSTYLESTEACHINGSOUND
CUSSIONMANAGINGWRITING
TYVENUECHORALSTYLESPERFORMANCE
REPERTOIREMODULATIONVOCALS
GCONDUCTINGADMINISTRATION
TINGPERCUSSIONDYNAMICSSCORING
VENUEVOCALSWRITINGPERCUSSION
ICALITIESPUBLICITYMUSIC
PERFORMANCEPRACTICALITIES
RT-UPTEACHINGCONDUCTING
YVENUECHORALSTYLESPERFORMANCE
MENTALSOUNDLIGHTING
INGDYNAMICSMANAGINGCHORAL
RT-UPTEACHINGCONDUCTING
RFORMANCEPRACTICALITIESMUSIC
MODULATIONSOUNDDYNAMICSSCORING
RATIONCONDUCTINGPUBLICITY
TIESSCORINGPLANNINGSTYLES
MANAGINGBARBERSHOPSTART-UP
NCEPRACTICALITIESMUSICSCORING
OUNDDYNAMICSMANAGINGBARBERSHOP
TINGSCORINGINSTRUMENTAL
DWRITINGPERCUSSIONMANAGING
DYNAMICSSTART-UPDYNAMICSCHORAL
TIONPUBLICITYPERCUSSIONVOCALS
GCONDUCTINGPERFORMANCEVENUE

PART I: STARTING OUT

DEMAND

The first thing to consider before starting your group is the market. Conduct some research – are there already three brass bands in your area? Does the other local choir rehearse on a Wednesday too? Do you have enough players to form a full wind band?

If you are a schoolteacher, don't be under any illusions about compulsory attendance. Unless it is a scheduled class, no child will ever attend any music practice on a regular basis unless they want to, and there will always be some reason not to: sport is the usual one, or you might clash with drama or dance or chess club; anything will do as an explanation for 'forgetting' to come. It is just as true for adults, of course: they will have babysitters failing to turn up, or children ill, or partners late home from work that night. In the end all that matters is whether they are with you rehearsing.

Amazingly, though, if you hit the right note with the type of group you create – in essence the 'product' – people will move mountains to ensure they are there with you.

THE PRODUCT

There are three factors:

- What you are offering
- What makes it different from other similar groups
- You.

What are you offering?

The major reason for this group's formation and continuing existence must be the music. While there may be numerous social aspects, you are not designing a community support group. Yes, it may function as one for some of the members (which is fantastic), but most people are there to make music and to get better at doing so.

What makes your group different?

It could be any number of things, but your group really needs to have a USP (unique selling point), at least at the start. This could be:

- Repertoire: are you the only one doing this style locally, or is it perhaps unique? It might be all your own music, or maybe even your own arrangements (see Parts IV and V).
- Financial: are you offering a better deal than other similar groups?
- Personnel: for example, is yours the only local group that does not require an audition?

You

Much of the success of your group will rely on your suitability for the role of leader. Ask yourself these questions:

1. What makes you certain you are the right person to direct this group?
2. Why would people want to spend time with you, and will there be enough of them to create an ensemble?

The fact is that you *are* the product. You will lead the group and choose the music for it; you will be the person at the front in all senses and everyone will see you as the key to the group's success or failure. To start with, people may well come along because of the music you are doing, but it is you, your leadership skills and your passion for the group that will keep them coming back.

Ask yourself a few more questions:

- Are you driven to create and lead this group, or is someone else persuading you to do it?
- Are you confident that you can do the musical aspects well enough?
- Do you have experience of this type of group, or a strong enough musical background to put you in a position to start a similar one?
- Do you enjoy the repertoire you are about to work on? You're going to spend a lot of time on it, certainly much more than your performers.
- Can you see any future for this group outside the rehearsal room?
- Are you the right person to do this at the moment? Maybe you could consider the possibility of working alongside someone else to gain experience before branching out on your own (rather in the manner of an assistant manager in a sports team).

Will people want to spend time with you?

Do you generally get on with people and know how to motivate them? Will you regard their levels of inexperience as a stimulating challenge or a continual source of frustration?

Imagine a conversation between two self-employed fathers, perhaps at the school gate:

> *'I've heard that [your name] is thinking of starting up a local community pop choir. I really like singing but I haven't been in a choir since school and I don't read music very well. Do you think it would be OK for me to go along?'*
>
> *'I should think so. [Your name] is good and patient and knows his stuff. He'll help you learn.'*
>
> *'Sounds great, and I'm free on Tuesday evenings. Perhaps I'll give it a try.'*

What would you expect/hope the response to be at this point? Will he come along to see what it is all about, mainly on the strength of your reputation and the music you are doing, or not? And will you get the same response at the end of similar conversations? It doesn't matter what actually happens from now on, it's what you believe will happen that is key: you have to trust yourself and your local musical reputation.

STANDARD ENSEMBLE TYPES

Listed below are the groups for which you are most likely to find commercially available written music. This does not preclude others of any combination – including a vocal/instrumental mix – but you may end up having to compose and arrange for these yourself.

Choral, using the standard abbreviations S(oprano), A(lto), T(enor), B(ass):

- SA/SSA – all female voices/boy trebles
- S(S)A men/SATB
- TTBB/barbershop.

Instrumental

- Wind band/concert band: wind, brass and percussion
- Brass band: brass and percussion
- Jazz orchestra/Big Band: saxophones, trumpets, trombones, rhythm section (piano, guitar, bass, drums and percussion)

- Orchestra: strings, wind, brass, percussion
- Clarinet/saxophone/flute choir
- Percussion ensemble: mix of tuned and untuned percussion.

In many ways it is easier to start up a choir than an instrumental group. However, that does not necessarily mean it is the right choice for you and, clearly, there are going to be more choirs than bands and orchestras as a result, leading to much greater scope for running instrumental groups.

Choral group

- Minimal access to accompaniment resources required: just a keyboard or backing track
- No need for anyone to read music except the director (although it will help – see Chapter 5)
- No need for written music at all – words may be sufficient at the start
- Wide variety of styles available
- No need for music stands
- Volume not really a problem – can be controlled if necessary
- Can be set up with relatively few people – two to three per part is enough.

Instrumental group

- Notated music needed
- Music stands needed
- Volume issues, particularly with brass and percussion
- Specific instrumental combinations required
- Each section needs a certain number of players to sound like a fullish band.

Once you have decided which type of ensemble you would like to go for, there are other factors to consider:

1. Who will be in the group?

- Pupils/children (for schoolteachers/youth workers)
- Friends and colleagues
- Musicians currently unknown to you.

2. What will be the age range?

- Young children: 5–10 years
- Teenagers/school age: 11–18

- Young adults/students: 19–23
- Adults: up to 70+.

Outside of a school environment it is unwise to mix the above age ranges – this is fraught with difficulties, both musical and social. Insurance/parental supervision can also be an issue with youngsters; aspects such as CRB checks, adult/child ratios and all elements of child safeguarding will need to be taken into account. Aim to set age limit rules and stick to them if possible.

3. Who is your likely audience?

- Friends and family
- Members of the public.

Should you audition or not?

Will your group be for everyone, or just the elite? The latter is not necessarily a bad thing – there may be many excellent musicians in your area crying out for the chance to do something challenging and rewarding, although you should perhaps explore why nobody else is doing it already before committing yourself. But if you want the best you're going to need to find them or at least invite them to join you.

Whichever type of group you opt for, there are advantages and disadvantages.

No auditions
Pros
- Should produce decent numbers relatively quickly.
- Less intimidating for potential members – they will not fear being 'the worst'.
- Strong sense of community spirit – 'all welcome'.
- Easier to replace leavers/absentees.

Cons
- Harder to attract and hold on to quality musicians – they may get bored/ frustrated by the slow speed you may need to work at for the majority.
- Can limit repertoire choices – there will be plenty of pieces you would like to do but cannot because they are too challenging. This can become an even bigger issue when the group members themselves suggest inappropriate repertoire.
- Can be tough to raise standards past a certain level (you should always aim higher than expected, but the weaknesses will still be there).
- Arguably more skills are required from you as a leader, as you must be able to motivate performers of all standards and levels of experience in the same rehearsal.

Auditioned/by invitation

Pros

- The repertoire available to you is much wider – you can do anything you like with the right personnel in front of you.
- Might be more satisfying for you as the director in the long run.
- Will make it easy to attract and hold on to good people, as they will want to be part of a quality group.
- You can feature certain individuals by deliberately selecting repertoire to highlight their skills. This will keep them interested (as well as the others who might see an opportunity for themselves in the future) and will also enable you to devise much more varied and imaginative concert programmes.
- High standards should be achieved and maintained, and subsequently your performances will be easier to sell, especially to the general public.

Cons

- It is much harder to find members and persuade them to come along. You might have specific people in mind, but they may not be available.
- It is tricky to find rehearsal slots – everyone is so busy and likely to be committed to multiple ensembles.
- You will need to organise regular performance opportunities. Decent players/ singers will not be interested in rehearsing without a specific goal in mind.
- It will be much harder to replace leavers.

WHEN SHOULD YOU MEET?

There are two elements for consideration: your needs and the needs of potential members.

Your needs

Pick a time you are happy with: you will be working hard during these practices and you don't want to find yourself resenting it because you have agreed to the wrong day of the week or an unsuitable time slot. Hopefully you will look forward to your sessions and experience a surge of adrenalin, but try to avoid times when, for whatever reason, you know you are likely to be tired or in a bad mood, such as after a regularly tedious meeting, or the longest working day of the week. Yet, the rehearsal may be just the thing to brighten your day. In the end you know how you will react in these scenarios, just make sure you are able to leave negative emotions outside the door of the rehearsal room.

The potential members of the group

The make-up of the group hinges on how important the musical/social balance is going to be. Are the members there to meet up or make music?

Is your rehearsal going to become a key part of their lives, something they look forward to every week, or is it just something else on their 'to do' list?

After considering the above aspects, you may end up with the following scenarios:

Rehearsals for non-auditioned adults/children and less experienced groups

- Once a week, same time, same day, same venue.
- Essential to develop rehearsal habit – 'Wednesday night is band night', or 'It's Friday lunchtime so it must be choir'.
- Social element is just as important as music. Your group is a place where the members meet up with like-minded people and develop strong, lasting friendships. This is true at any age, and you need to encourage this sense of camaraderie and identity by building in coffee breaks/chat time.

Auditioned/by invitation

These are likely to be a very different group of people who are there for the music. They will be busy, and will also inevitably be involved in a number of music groups on a weekly basis. Many of them may also be travelling from some distance.

But they will come if the product is good and different from anything else on offer: ideally the opportunity to perform exciting, challenging and unusual repertoire with good players/singers. Of course, there is still a social element – there must be – but it is not the prime reason they are there.

So, with this in mind, aim for the following for this type of group:

- Rehearsal bookings anything from once a fortnight down to two or three times per year, ideally leading to a specific performance/event.
- With less frequent rehearsals, ensure you warn the members well in advance, and aim for the same slots every year if you can.
- Select the repertoire early and publicise it: the music choice is one of the major reasons they are coming.

HOW LONG SHOULD REHEARSALS BE?

As always this depends on a number of factors, the most obvious of which are specific time constraints. Many of these will occur naturally in a school/office environment. If there is only an hour lunch break and you assume that few people are likely to arrive in the first ten minutes of that hour and need to be released early to get to their next appointment of lesson, then you are left with around 50 minutes at best. This is not ideal and will influence your choice of repertoire, but it is beyond your control. If you do have the luxury of choosing the length of your rehearsals, there are several factors to take into account:

- The age and experience of the members
- The lifestyle of the members (or their parents), and the time and distance travelled to and from the venue
- The amount of rehearsal time (not counting breaks) which you feel you require to deliver the chosen repertoire to a good standard.

The age and experience of the members

As a rule, most youngsters' concentration spans are finite and they are unlikely to be effective much past 45 minutes without a break (ideally involving fresh air and a brief change of scenery). This is especially true for young brass and wind players whose lips will be suffering after less than half an hour in some cases (see Chapter 6). Inexperienced adult performers are no different, especially if they are finding the repertoire challenging – they will need a break for a chat and a refurbishment of the blood sugar levels. This can be particularly relevant as the group nears a concert performance. As the leader, you will have so much to get through (see Chapter 7) that you will almost certainly be tempted to drive your charges into the ground, but try to remember breaks if you can.

Lifestyles

When deciding on a time and length for your rehearsal, try to envisage who will be coming and where your practice might fit into their day. In many ways the school/office lunchtime rehearsal is the easiest to run: any potential members may be busy, but at least they will be on site. Compare that with the busy parent aiming to be in several places at the same time, only one of which is the pick-up after your rehearsal at 5.30 p.m. Or, if your target market is a community choir for young mothers, when is the most likely time they will be able to leave the house once their partner/babysitter is on the scene? Is 7 p.m. really a viable start time, or would 7.30/7.45 make their lives so much easier?

How long will it take the group to learn the music?

This is crucial. Nobody else can tell you how long it will take your ensemble to learn something to performance standard, but you really ought to know. Are you making assumptions, for instance that all your members will be able/ willing to turn up to extra, emergency rehearsals if you start running out of time?

Take the following factors into account:

- Do any of the pieces need to be staged?
- Will outsiders (such as soloists) need to be slotted in, and how soon?
- How often will you need to practise in the performance location, apart from on the day?
- Who will your audience be, and what level of performance will they expect of your group? (See below.)

Assuming that your members are not semi-professional, aim for between an hour and an hour and a half, with a break included. By all means try a two-hour slot, but you will probably need more than one break to compensate. There are times you will want to do less than an hour, especially if you are feeling under the weather, but remember that some of your members may have travelled significant distances to be with you that night, quite possibly having given up other commitments or family time, and they deserve a full rehearsal. You don't want them driving home and calculating that they will have spent longer in the car than with you.

ADDITIONAL PEOPLE: CAN YOU DO ALL THIS YOURSELF OR WILL YOU NEED HELP?

You probably can do this by yourself, but only at the start. While the group is small you can easily do any administration (see Chapter 2), but as it gets bigger it will become less realistic for you to manage this on top of looking after the musical side. Especially at amateur level, you are bound to find a number of competent, willing helpers who will be only too pleased to take registers, collect money and organise any social events.

Surprisingly, despite the fact that a choir is often easier to start up than a band, you are more likely to need someone alongside you for the former. It all depends how confident you are as a pianist/guitarist, and whether you are happy to take rehearsals and play at the same time. Some conductors prefer to do it themselves while others will opt to have a rehearsal pianist so they can be in front of the choir as much as possible.

Bear in mind that, if you usually accompany your own group at choir sessions, you may need to find someone else to do it when it comes to public performance: someone who is capable, fully understands the genre of music that you are doing and can deliver it to your satisfaction. Hopefully this newcomer will enhance the performance, but they will not be you and you must be prepared to accept that.

This will not apply if you use a backing track in performance, of course, and you might even consider the possibility of recording your own piano/guitar track for your choir to sing over. Or you could just risk playing anyway, confident in the knowledge that your choir will deliver without you at the front to inspire them. Whatever your preferred solution – and it will often be linked to the type of event you are putting on – it is vital that you ensure the performance is not compromised in any way.

For instrumental groups you should be fine on your own, although with an orchestra it may be worth ensuring that you have a strong leader (first violin). This is especially true with inexperienced groups where one high-quality player in a key role can make all the difference: the equivalent might be the lead trumpet/saxophone in a jazz orchestra. Such a player guarantees decent playing in both the rehearsal and the performance, and it can be very useful to have a more experienced musician to talk to when things are not going as well as you had hoped. Leading a group can be isolating and it is often difficult to see for yourself when (and why) things aren't going well. Having someone experienced on hand, who you can trust to set you back on the right track or rein you in if necessary, is essential.

Use of backing tracks

There are many commercially-available backing tracks, although they vary in quality, so you need to do your research. The benefits are obvious – when your choir performs, the singers feel as if they are with a full instrumental ensemble, with all its requisite power and orchestral colour. However, there are also limitations: the tempo is dictated to you, as is the key, and you are forced to perform the piece at full length. This last aspect can be a drawback, especially when you are given a time limit for a performance and you are forced to reject a song simply because it is too long.

PERFORMANCE STANDARDS: HOW GOOD WILL YOUR GROUP NEED TO BE?

This is worth considering at an early stage. You must be realistic when you are working with young people or inexperienced adults: they will try their best but they will make mistakes. This does not mean that you should not attempt to get them to perform as well as possible, but if they do not reach the perfection for which you are searching, do not be overly concerned.

Try this as a golden rule:

Your group should always be just a little bit better than the audience is expecting.

Remember, the audience members are on your side and, in many cases, will be related in some way to the performers anyway. They are not looking to criticise, they are just thrilled to see their mum/dad/son/daughter/partner taking part in something worthwhile and clearly thriving on the opportunity. As the leader you will know how well the performance has gone and what needs to be improved, but you should also be able to acknowledge how well everyone has done, especially if the group has been together for only a relatively short space of time. And that word 'time' is key: there should be no rush with a group like this. As long as they feel proud of themselves they will keep coming, and that will give you the chance to help them improve. Don't underestimate the effect of the members' enjoyment on the overall performance. Such an emotion is infectious, among both themselves and the audience, and is much more powerful than you might think.

Performance levels and context

In general, think of the need to attain perfection in direct correlation to the performance circumstances you encounter: they are not all the same. In essence there are four[†] scenarios, starting with the easiest.

A. Performance outdoors with audience milling about/wandering past

This is what happens at most outdoors public events – anywhere in fact where your group is providing entertainment but is not the main attraction. In many ways the visual presentation is more important than the music here, as without decent (and expensive) amplification little detail will be heard and a complex wind band piece may be reduced to a drum beat, tuba bass line and occasional piercing flute.

However, this does not make such a performance opportunity worthless; far from it, as it takes the pressure off and allows everyone to relax and try out new repertoire. You can chat to your performers in between numbers, and even sing/whistle missing entries if necessary – nobody else will know. This is the chance to take risks, secure in the knowledge that nobody will really mind.

B. Performance outdoors with seated audience

Whether in a marquee, town square or the middle of a field, much of the detail of the performance will inevitably be lost and dynamic contrast will be rendered ineffective. Unless everything is carefully miked up, any sophistication in the arrangement will be neutralised. All those harmonies and

---

† A fifth category – positioned somewhere between C and D – might be 'Performance in competition', perhaps as part of a festival. However, any leader putting his/her ensemble into this situation should know what is required of the group by then.

countermelodies are all very well but, in the end, the audience will want to hear the tune. The key difference from scenario A is that the audience is there specifically to see your group.[†]

C. Performance indoors with seated audience

This is much more pressurised and intense as everything can be heard. Your group is also very much the centre of attention, as the audience is there to listen to it at that moment in time and can reasonably expect to hear every detail. The atmosphere will usually be formal, expectations will be relatively high, and there is very much the sense of an 'event' taking place.

D. Recording

This is undoubtedly the toughest requirement as, unlike all the others, the performance will be heard again and again and those mistakes will never go away. Over time the errors will become part of the music, but it is worth taking the trouble to eliminate them during the recording and production process. The repertoire must be carefully chosen, and should ideally have been performed in public several times before the recording date.

Logically you should aim to work up through these performance scenarios. However, this is not always possible – for example, scheduling an outdoor performance in the middle of January is not wise, and it is unlikely that your group will be invited to perform at a school fete until it is more established.

There is also an issue of repertoire and how much time you need to fill. You cannot agree to fill half an hour until you have learned enough music to a sufficient standard; in the case of a pop 'covers' choir that could easily be ten three-minute songs. The audience will be supportive, but there is a limit, so think carefully before accepting a booking or it may be your last.

Leading an ensemble can be scary at times, but it is also exciting and immensely creative. To commit to a venture like this you must be the right sort of person, someone who is prepared to speculate to accumulate, even someone who is prepared to fail in extreme cases. It will not be easy, and your group is unlikely to develop in a nice straight line graph: there will be setbacks along the way. However, there will also be triumphs, anything from

---

† If your choir is invited to perform outdoors, particularly when you have no opportunity to pre-rehearse on the stage, it might be wise to do at least part of a previous rehearsal outdoors as well so the singers get some idea of the acoustic (or lack of it) that they will face. This is especially important with inexperienced singers who may well be shocked by how little they can hear themselves or their colleagues.

great feedback after a good rehearsal to victory in local and even national competitions.

Starting up and running a musical ensemble is not for everyone, and certainly not for those who love their comfort zones, but for an experienced solo musician such as yourself, it is the logical next step, an opportunity to give something back. As André Previn says, taking the easy option is not always wise or fulfilling:

'I have always found it necessary for my work to scare me. It doesn't do any good to be totally secure in the knowledge that tomorrow's efforts will not be too difficult and that they will, with rare exception, be accepted with praise.'

(Previn, 1993)

The following chapter addresses the practicalities of running your group.

Founder: Cliff van Tonder; Band Leader: Georgi Bartlett
www.elmbridgebigband.co.uk

What is the ensemble?
The Elmbridge Community Big Band is a non-auditioned, non-profit community big band with charitable status. The group was formed in August 2009 by the founder of the Elmbridge Choir and Ladies' Choir, Cliff van Tonder, and is part of the Elmbridge Community Music Society (ECMS).

IN THE BEGINNING

Who did you expect your audience to be?
Mainly local residents and people who were already connected to the choirs and other ensembles within ECMS.

Why did you want to do it?
Our vision was of creating a band with a relaxed and fun atmosphere where we could make great music but also make great friends at the same time.

What were your criteria for success? Did you have a one-year/five-year plan?
- Positive attitude to leadership with flexibility to encompass the feelings of the members of the band.
- Good music scores – mixing up simple music with challenging pieces.
- Lots of practice (individually and as a group and sectionals).
- Social time as a group.
- Set regular goals, both in terms of musical aspects and fundraising.

Advertising: how did you do it?
The charity board includes a publicity secretary, giving us access to slots in the local papers and online as well as flyers in town halls and similar community points, including local radio.

THE ONGOING PROCESS

Do you audition?
Not to join the band, but we do audition for our vocalists.

Venue: how and why did you choose it?
Local to where other sections of our charity rehearse, large room and low fees to keep costs down.

Practice times: when, and for how long?
Weekly for two hours: Tuesdays 8–10 p.m.

Funding: what system do you have?
We have charity status so a financial officer looks after our accounts.

Do you have any assistants at rehearsals?
No, although the more experienced musicians help out the less experienced players when needed.

What about administration?
Day-to-day admin is all run through the website which the members can log on to, including rehearsal updates and concert information.

To what extent has your original plan changed?
Not a huge amount of change – we are more selective now on numbers allowed in each section than at the start (purely to preserve the balance).

What advice would you give to someone else considering a similar venture?
Think very clearly about the direction you want to take your group, and have a plan and stick to it.

FOR THE CONDUCTOR

What three key tips can you pass on about organising/taking ensemble rehearsals?
- Keep it fun – musically and in terms of how you approach rehearsing.
- Keep it challenging – people will leave if they do not feel they are improving and gaining something from the experience.
- Keep it pacy to maintain respect and interest in the group.

And in performance?
- Never let them know you're nervous.
- Take it slow between pieces – some audience banter can earn some precious recovery time.

Who are your musical heroes?
James Galway, saxophonist Candy Dulfer and the Glenn Miller Orchestra.

TAL CHORAL STYLES ARRANGING
PLANNING VENUE VOCALS DYNAMICS
G CONDUCTING ADMINISTRATION
TY VENUE SOUND DYNAMICS MANAGING
—UP TEACHING CONDUCTING LIGH
RFORMANCE PRACTICALITIES
UCTING   TY
Y VENUE DYNAMICS MANAGING CHORAL
PERCUSSION INSTRUMENTAL
IP LIGHTING SCORING STYLES

CASE STUDY:
ROADE COMMUNITY ORCHESTRA

Musical Director: Ian Riley; Administrator: Tim Chisholm
www.roadecommunityorchestra.com

Who are you?
The Roade Community Orchestra, Northants (formed in 1999).

What is the ensemble?
Having started as an evening class with about ten people playing a variety
of instruments it is now about 35–40 strong. We evolved from being a local
authority evening class because of the increased cost and to take charge of
our own destiny. There were three strong members at that stage to form a
committee and, along with the MD, we established the goal of a cheap and
independent chance to play ensemble music. The MD approached the local
primary school for a venue, and I had worked with the local music service and
been successful with lottery grants so I followed up the charitable status angle
(which I strongly recommend). We cut the costs to members by more than 50%
to a subscription of about £20 per term.

IN THE BEGINNING

Who did you expect your audience to be?
Audience was not a great issue in the early stages, it was the ensemble itself
that was the main aim, with the possibility of supporting some village events.

Why did you want to do it?
Most of the then small group had the chance to play music with their children
and others. I, for example, had the chance to play the trumpet again after 25
years.

What is/was your unique selling point?
All abilities were welcome, as the MD would write music and differentiate for all
abilities. It is all about enjoyment and ensemble playing, although the general
ability improves as we succeed.

What were your criteria for success?
Financial independence and growth of numbers.

Advertising: how did you do it?
Through local music teachers, flyers, posters in libraries and word of mouth.
The website was a later addition.

THE ONGOING PROCESS

Do you audition?
No.

Venue: how and why did you choose it?
The school we use is central to the village and the hall has good acoustics
and offers a decent concert venue. There is ample parking, a supportive head
teacher, and it is good for the school to be part of a community group.

Funding: what system do you have?
Termly subscriptions, with family discount. Gift aid is a major part of keeping
the subs low. We raise further monies through concerts, carol singing and have
had a few local sponsors in the past.

Do you have any assistants at rehearsals?
For the first two years we had a string teacher join us.

What about administration?
All done through the committee.

To what extent has your original plan changed?
We started by encouraging children of all ages to join us and experience
ensemble playing, which also helped to raise funds. We now have very few
children and the age/ability has risen considerably.

What difficulties have you encountered?
Finance; children improving then leaving to join county groups; work
commitments.

What advice would you give to someone else considering a similar venture?
Concentrate on the ensemble not the audience initially. There are some
stunning musicians out there who have lost confidence, and they need a lot of
nurturing.

TALCHORALSTYLESARRANGING
PLANNINGVENUEVOCALSDYNAMICS
GCONDUCTINGADMINISTRATION
TYVENUESOUNDDYNAMICSMANAGING
-UPTEACHINGCONDUCTING IGH
RFORMANCEPRACTI
UCTINGSCORINGTE
YVENUEDYNAMICSMA CHORAL
PERCUSSIONINSTRUMENTAL
IPLIGHTINGSCORING

CHAPTER 2:
PRACTICALITIES AND
PUBLICITY

ATTRACTING MEMBERS

Your great idea will work only if you can persuade people to join you, and
that means they have to know about it. There are plenty of ways to advertise,
of course, but not until you have ascertained exactly what you want any
prospective members to know.

Advertising

Most of us can manipulate a Word document or even specific design software
well enough to produce a decent poster, but it is the concept, layout and
content that are hard to get right. Get it wrong and you end up attracting either
the wrong people or nobody at all.

In a sense we are jumping the gun here – is everything absolutely sorted out? If
not, make sure it is before telling anyone else about it – you really cannot afford
any confusion at such an early stage in your group's development.

Let's take a step back. What do you need to know?

- The style of music you are going to do
- The venue
- The day and time
- A name would be nice, although it could come later.

The musical style

You may well know exactly what you are going to do, but can you put it into
words? Descriptions such as 'glam rock' or 'New Romantic' might mean everything to you but comparatively little to anyone else. Instrumental music is even
harder: what does 'classical' mean to most people? Probably not the era of
Mozart and Beethoven anyway – it has become such a catch-all term. And what
is 'swing music'? Ellington and Basie? Glenn Miller? Or just jazz in general? If
possible, without cluttering up your poster too much, it is a good idea to offer
a few specific titles if you can, or perhaps artists. 'Featuring the music of Elton
John, Abba and Queen' sends a pretty clear message.

The venue

This is a crucial decision, with potentially far-reaching consequences. Let's imagine you are planning to rehearse your choir and you are offered the use of a drama studio – this isn't as good as it might seem. One word: curtains. Anywhere used for dramatic purposes will have been designed to have almost no echo to emphasise the clarity of the spoken word; perfect for speaking, disastrous for singing. However, a room can also be *too* resonant, especially for the crisp rhythmic requirements of a jazz orchestra, for example.

So, the choice of venue matters a great deal, especially at the start of the process. No matter what the group, your first job is to get the members to feel positive about the sound they are making, and for that you need a decent acoustic. On the plus side, drama studio curtains will brilliantly 'kill' the sound of a rock drum kit, resulting in a crisp, clear-cut sound which will balance well with the amplified vocalist. Sadly, it will just as effectively kill any resonance produced by a choir or brass band, and everyone will leave their first rehearsal feeling depressed, believing that they are much worse than they actually are – not a great start!

Venue: other aspects to consider

- **Access and parking:** is it easy to find and reach? Is there disabled access? How far is the hall from the car park? (Think pouring rain in November – will people be put off coming that night?)
- **Hire cost:** how much is it and what are you getting for your money?
- **Equipment provided:** is there a piano/keyboard, or will you need to bring your own equipment?
- **Space:** it may be ideal for 15–20 at the moment, but try to think bigger than this – how many people are you realistically hoping for in the longer term? Will they still fit comfortably? You don't want to move venue if you can help it.
- **Chairs:** are there enough and are they the right type? Adults are not going to be very happy sitting on primary school chairs or benches for an hour and, in a school, the 'big' chairs may not be so easy to get at.
- **Music stands:** are they provided, or will the players need to bring their own?
- **Toilets:** are they guaranteed to be open and easily accessible?

The key is to shop around. Your chosen venue does not have to be a purpose-built sound studio. Primary and secondary schools are a good start, although not necessarily the main halls – they may charge less for the use of the music room instead. Church halls, community centres, disused buildings – use your imagination and contacts, and let people know you are looking. Do not just take the first venue offered to you. It may be nearby, or even at your place of work, but that does not necessarily make it a good choice. The friend who has offered you the use of the disused chapel free of charge will have done it with the best of intentions, but you know that your proposed percussion samba group will sound dreadful in there, so politely decline and keep looking. And you must do a site visit, of course – don't take someone else's word for it.

Even though your community choir will probably never sound like The King's Singers no matter how long you rehearse in the local parish church, if you get the venue correct it will go a long way to encouraging the success of your new group in its early stages.

To hire or not to hire?

For the reasons outlined above it is not always best to take the free option. In any case, paying is not such a bad idea, provided the members are prepared to make a contribution.

FEES

Whether you wish to be paid for your time depends on your circumstances and your reasons for embarking on this project in the first place. Clearly if you are a full-time, salaried professional running a percussion group on a Monday evening, and you are fortunate to have access to a suitable venue free of charge, you may not see a need for financial reward and will be more than happy to do it for the love of it.

However, if you are a freelancer (such as a peripatetic instrumental teacher) then this is a key part of your livelihood and you need to make this clear to everyone at the start. Whatever your situation, at the very least it is advisable to ensure that your costs are covered to avoid leaving yourself out of pocket. You will inevitably incur expenses such as music purchase and venue hire, so these will need to be covered in some way.

Some possible models to consider are discussed below.

A. The full membership scheme

- Every member pays for a standard number of rehearsals up front, regardless of whether they attend all sessions. This covers the rent, new music, band uniforms, the purchase of unusual instruments and so on.

This is a standard approach, and it is very much weighted towards you and not the members. In theory it should make your life easier, both financially and musically. You are pretty much guaranteed to get a full group every night, which should make rehearsal schedules much easier to design.

However, this group is made up only of those who can comfortably pay a substantial amount of money in advance two or three times a year, and can commit to being available every week. How many more members might you be missing out on who do not have either of those options? Might they be persuaded to join if you offered a slightly more flexible approach? Perhaps a fairer option might be the retainer scheme.

B. The retainer scheme

- You set a standard fee per session, £7.50 for example, payable on the night.
- All members agree to pay a percentage up front as a retainer, 40% for example, regardless of whether they attend or not.
- Those who attend on the night agree to top up to the full session fee.

This works in two ways: you can guarantee to cover your costs every week because you have sufficient funding in advance, and every member has at least invested something in the venture so feels some sense of commitment. However, if for some reason they are unable to come for a particular week they have only lost 40% of the fee for that night.

This approach is a happy medium.

You may even be able to combine models A and B to produce a third model:

C. The option scheme (with incentives)

- Members are given the choice as to whether to pay the full amount in advance *or* opt for the retainer approach.
- Those who agree to pay up front will be entitled to a reduction, perhaps 10%.
- Those who opt for the retainer understand that they will be expected to top up to the full session fee every time they attend, so may end up paying more than those who pay up front. However, they still have a considerable element of flexibility.
- The whole process is managed discretely to avoid any embarrassment.

This would seem to be an ideal solution: those who can afford to pay the full amount in advance will, those who cannot are not obliged to do so. You can easily cover your costs with plenty to spare.

However, there is still a financial commitment involved, albeit reduced, so some people may still be put off from joining. There is a fourth approach, as follows.

D. Payment at the session

- Anyone who turns up pays a flat fee.
- If they do not/cannot appear for whatever reason, they do not pay.

Here the members have all the power and it is clearly risky for you: one low turnout and you will not break even that week. However, such a 'free' approach might lead to more people appearing in the long run as they will not feel under any obligation. It will be purely their decision on the night, and many more might come along to give it a try as a result.

The major difficulty arises when you are trying to teach repertoire without any knowledge of who will/will not be there from week to week: how many cellos will you get tonight, if any? What if the key solo soprano doesn't show up today? Will this piece work without a rhythm section?

There are numerous variations on the above approaches, but as long as you can pay the rent every week and feel that your time is valued, that is all that matters.

Income

Depending on the kind of model you opt for, you may begin to generate a level of profit that can be used to benefit the group as a whole, for example:

- Social events such as meals or outings, subsidised by group finances.
- Equipment to make the members' lives easier, such as music stands kept at the venue to save them having to bring their own.
- Better advertising of your performances, such as glossier posters or the purchasing of advertising in the local press, and so on.
- Band/choir uniforms with logos, ensuring a sense of style and group identity.
- Hiring a part-time PA/press secretary to deal with the administration. This might even be someone from within the group.

Additionally, unless you are planning to write or arrange everything yourself, over time you should aim to own everything rather than borrowing or hiring. In this way you will always be building up the group's music library, and you can never have too much decent music.

INSURANCE

Make sure you as an individual have insurance. Few public venues will accept you as the official hirer without insurance, and be certain that you are insured by a reputable company, ideally one which specialises in the performing arts. The key is that everyone in your care should be covered if they are injured in the process of working on your behalf. This may not just be during regular rehearsals but also at any private and public events where your group might be performing. If you have asked them to take part, they are your responsibility; do not expect the venue or event itself to be covered. As always with insurance, assume nothing and check the small print. Be aware that there are different rules governing children under 16, so this may affect your choice of age group to work with. This particularly applies to the number of designated adults required when travelling on coaches and so on. If in doubt, always check with your insurer.

THE ADVERTISING CAMPAIGN

Once you have considered all of the practicalities outlined above you will be ready to create your advertising campaign to attract members to your exciting new venture.

On the next page is an example of a poster designed for the relaunch of the Stage Choir at High Wycombe Music Centre. A brief analysis of this poster raises the following points:

- It is too busy, mainly as a result of trying to convey all the repertoire information and general appeal to as many children as possible. Subsequent versions were simplified.
- There is a deliberately informal approach at the top, aimed at the target market. If they understand the language they are more likely to be interested and spread the word.
- The leader's name is seen as a prospective selling point. For instance, a former long-serving Head of Music in the area should add credibility.
- The age limit is clearly visible.
- Time and location are clear.
- Contact details are evident. These could have been personal details (email and mobile number only, of course, never an address) but in this case the county music office contacts were appropriate.
- A website might help – anything that enables people to confirm your credibility and experience.

What about a start date?

In this example that question would have been answered centrally by the county music staff, but without that luxury it will have to go on the poster. Be sure to update your poster as the date begins to look old if you are still recruiting new members later on.

*Do you enjoy 'X Factor' and 'Britain's Got Talent'
but secretly believe you could do better?*

*Do your friends keep insisting you
stop singing along to your iPod?*

*Are you a frustrated 'shower' singer,
eager to take the next step?*

Then why not join

STAGE CHOIR

Directed by Patrick Gazard

**Music from shows and films:
Sweeney Todd, Five Guys Named Moe, Moulin Rouge
and
Billy Elliot for 2011.**

Opportunities for soloists as well as full choir

And it's for boys as well – plenty for the guys to do...

No auditions – just come along and see what you think

When? 10.45–11.45 a.m. Saturday Mornings
Who? Anyone aged 12 and above is welcome.
Where? Room 9, Millbrook Combined School, Mill End Rd,
High Wycombe HP12 4BA

Contact us
Tel 01494 xxxxxx;
Email hwmusic@buckscc.gov.uk;
Website www.buckscc.gov.uk/hwmc

Other advertising approaches:

- Press release/advert: this will cost you, but should reach a lot of people as a result. Just make sure that the readers are the target market.
- Social networking: there is no faster or more efficient way to let your community know about something, especially as it starts to grow. Encourage all your starter members to put the word out immediately.

The practicalities of setting up a new musical group may not be that exciting or especially creative, but it is worth spending time on them at this early stage. Having everything firmly in place before the first session, while allowing for some flexibility and change later on, should stand you in good stead and allow you to concentrate on the music.

TAL CHORAL STYLES ARRANGING
PLANNING VENUE VOCALS DYNAMICS
G CONDUCTING ADMINISTRATION
TY VENUE SOUND DYNAMICS MANAGING
—UP TEACHING CONDUCTING LIG
RFORMANCE PRACTICALITIES
UCTIN   IN   U
Y VENUE DYNAMICS MANAGING CHORAL
PERCUSSION INSTRUMENTAL
IP LIGHTING SCORING STYLES

www.thebachchoir.org.uk

Who are you?
David Hill, Musical Director of the Bach Choir. Also Chief Conductor of the
BBC Singers/Musical Director of Leeds Philharmonic Society, Associate Guest
Conductor of Bournemouth Symphony Orchestra and Musical Director of
Southern Sinfonia

What is the ensemble?
The Bach Choir was created in 1876, and I am its 9th Musical Director, following
in the footsteps of Vaughan Williams, Holst and Willcocks. It is a mixed adult
choir made up of singers from all walks of life and has been described by the
London Evening Standard as 'probably the finest independent choir in the
world'.

IN THE BEGINNING

What were your criteria for success? Did you have a one-year/five-year plan?
High standards in programming and in concerts. We plan several years ahead
with an overview of how things should be progressing.

Advertising: how did you do it?
We employ a PR agency.

THE ONGOING PROCESS

Do you audition?
Yes, the entry audition is of a high standard, thereafter triennially or sooner if
needed.

Venue: how and why did you choose it?
Westminster Cathedral Hall. This is a long-standing tradition as the choir has rehearsed there for over 100 years.

Practice times: when, and for how long?
Monday evenings from 18:15–20:15. Sessions are sometimes extended depending on workload.

Funding: what system do you have?
Subscriptions/friends' schemes/trusts.

Do you have any assistants at rehearsals?
A pianist who acts as assistant conductor.

What about administration?
We have a full-time professional administrator supported by volunteers from the choir and a clearly designed management structure.

To what extent has your original plan changed?
Substantially – we are now a much more professional organisation.

What difficulties have you encountered?
Following the loss of a permanent sponsor, our funding is now more diverse.

What advice would you give to someone else considering a similar venture?
A financial plan is imperative as public money is now in very short supply.

What three key tips can you pass on about organising ensemble rehearsals?
The three 'E's: Efficiency, Energy and Enthusiasm.

And a tip for performances?
You should attempt to show something about the music no one had realised until that point.

PART II:
CONDUCTING AND REPERTOIRE

'[Conducting is] the direction of a musical performance by visible gestures designed to secure unanimity of execution and interpretation.'
(Grove Concise Dictionary of Music, 1988)

'Conducting is like holding a small bird in your hand. If you hold it too tightly you crush it; if you hold it too loosely it flies away.'
Sir Colin Davis, quoted as advice to Charles Hazelwood in his lecture 'Trusting the Ensemble' (www.ted.com)

When conducting, the most important thing is the music that results from your direction. If you only ever conduct one group, provided they understand your various gestures, even unorthodox methods will work just fine.

Your primary aim is to keep everyone on the same musical track while also enabling them to express themselves and their individual musical personalities. It is a challenging balancing act to achieve and it takes years of practice, but when it works there is nothing better. Essentially, the ideal sound in your head is being reproduced in front of you and communicated to an audience.

In practical terms, your role is to:

- Provide a clear beat
- Set the tempo, including any changes
- Indicate/cue important entries
- Communicate and interpret the phrasing and dynamics
- Convey the mood and style of the music.

Bearing in mind the importance of first impressions (Chapter 5), you can develop the role as you see fit with your own style, but understanding the basics of conducting will give your group confidence in you. A decent conducting technique may also encourage the more experienced musicians to stay.

BEATING TIME

Beginners should visit the companion website to this book for an explanation of the mechanics of beating time.

Setting the tempo

Assuming you are not using backing tracks, you will need to set the speed of the piece, not only at the start but anywhere it changes. Getting the tempo right sounds so simple, but it is arguably the toughest and most vital part of your job, especially in performance. Go too fast (adrenalin is a dangerous thing) and nobody will be able to play it. However, going too slowly can also cause problems: it is not the speed the performers are expecting and that unsettles everyone. A piece can rush or it can drag, and sometimes it is out of your control anyway – an insufficiently rehearsed rhythm section that picks its own speed can cause havoc. And yet, when you and your group get the tempo right, everything seems effortless – you have found the natural speed of the music.

So how do I know what speed a piece should go at?
Clearly your best guide is the metronome mark (e.g. ♩ = 120), but even that might be wrong, or at least wrong for your group. It is, however, much more use than a vague 'allegro' or 'andante' marking. A quick glance at any metronome will reveal the wide variety of options open to you, not to mention the different interpretations of these Italian terms through the ages. It can also depend on the type of music. You would expect to hear every note of a stately dance, whereas a lively musical theatre medley finale may be much more about panache and energy than right notes. Avoid the temptation to take a fast movement slowly – it never works. If it cannot be played at close to the correct speed, don't choose it for your group (see Chapter 4).

Setting the correct tempo under performance conditions takes practice and, even then, you may not get it right every time. In general, if a piece is meant to be played fast try to ensure it feels fast to the listener, and vice versa for a slow work. Persevere, always use your ears to hear what is actually happening in front of you, and never give up trying to find that elusive 'ideal' speed. Even the greatest leaders find it tricky – witness conductor André Previn reminiscing about the relative value of the Oscars he has won for his film scores:

'My Academy Award statuettes stand in the corner of a bookcase ... of course it would have been much more valuable if I had been given the unassailably correct tempos for the major works of Mozart as a prize.'

(Previn, 1993)

Does it matter how many beats/bars in I give?
Many conductors would tell you that you only need a single upbeat to bring
in an ensemble entry. This may well be true with an experienced director
and an equally experienced ensemble, but at amateur level it is fraught with
danger. If you lack the confidence to get it right your performers will sense your
uncertainty, and this is unlikely to result in a clean and convincing entry.

So, at least in the early stages, do not be frightened to beat half a bar for
nothing, or even a whole bar in some cases. At fast tempi such as a one-in-a-
bar waltz or an energetic $\frac{6}{8}$ Scottish reel you may even opt for the safety of two
bars for nothing.

The rules are simple. It does not matter what you choose to do, provided that:

- Your 'bar for nothing' is done at the same speed as the upcoming entry
- Everyone knows what you are going to do *in advance*
- You actually remember to do it in the performance.

Consistency is the key: a conductor who gives two bars for nothing in rehearsal
and then spontaneously decides that one bar will do for the performance
is a menace. By all means experiment with different approaches during the
rehearsal process, but make sure everything is set in stone at least a fortnight
before the performance itself.

Should I use a baton?
That is entirely up to you. It is more common for choral conductors to forgo the
baton than instrumental, but there are plenty of notable exceptions. Musical
style can also be a guide – jazz and rock are not really baton friendly.

The only occasions where a baton might be deemed essential is when your
performers have difficulty in seeing you otherwise. This may happen when you
are directing a theatrical 'pit' band, or possibly a major work for chorus and
orchestra where the back row of singers is a considerable distance away from
you. However, you are unlikely to meet either of these scenarios in the early
stages of your conducting career.

In the end it is your choice, and you should do whichever feels most
comfortable or natural to you.

Are there different conducting techniques for different musical genres?
Much of the conductor's role is exactly the same in any style, as defined in
the Grove quote at the beginning of the chapter, so logically the gestures and

indications will be very similar. However, there are differences as well, as we will see below.

Conducting to backing tracks: is there any point?
With backing tracks much of the work is done for you whether you like it or not. Everything should happen like clockwork and it will be exactly the same every time. There are no issues with tempo and ensemble.

This is ideal, as it allows you to concentrate purely on the singers. Your role now is to bring them in, control their dynamics, and so on, safe in the knowledge that the 'band' is secure. Consequently, you and your singers should be able to pay close attention to detail. Note though that you may find it frustrating when your dynamic contrasts are not mirrored in the pre-recorded track.

Conducting jazz and rock – is it different from the 'classical' approach?
In most cases, songs in these styles will be driven by a rhythm section, the engine room of the band. You will need to spend plenty of time working with these key players (see Chapter 6) but it will be time well spent, as you will then be able to leave them to it and concentrate on the ensemble instruments. Try not to over-conduct in these styles. However, clarifying any accompanying figures is a good idea, especially if they are marked 'on cue', which is to say when the conductor says so!

What does the conductor's left hand do[†]?
If it was up to the composer and conductor Richard Strauss, the answer would be very straightforward:

'The left hand has nothing to do with conducting. Its proper place is in the waistcoat pocket from which it should only emerge to restrain or to make some minor gesture for which in any case a scarcely perceptible glance would suffice.'

(Strauss, quoted in *Larousse*, 1982)

This is all very amusing, but there is a serious point here. Waving the left hand aimlessly is meaningless, and 'mirror conducting' is futile, apart from at certain major moments. Indeed, assuming your conducting technique is reasonably clear, one hand should be sufficient. So was Strauss correct, or are there other ways of looking at this dilemma?

'The stick is the beat; the other hand is the musician.'
(Donald Runnicles, Conductor of BBC Scottish Symphony Orchestra)

---

† Left-handers should experiment with either hand to see which feels more comfortable.

'The baton hand is for the grammar and the other is for the poetry.'
(Peter Stark, Professor of Conducting, Royal College of Music)

In other words, merely beating in time does not produce good music: it is the *result* that matters. Your beating may be small and neat for some styles of music, and large and expansive for others.

Your left hand should shape the music. Ebbs and flows, phrasing, dynamic contrasts – all of these come from the left hand. A good conductor must be able to do different things with both hands simultaneously, and it takes practice to achieve this. You communicate the music through the way you behave on the stage, and this will be transmitted to the performers. Thus it follows that if you send unintentional messages to your singers and players, they will perform the music in a specific (and incorrect) way.

What is subdivision, and why is it used?
Subdivision is beating shorter note values than the time signature implies, in order to achieve tighter, cleaner ensemble. Examples might be:

- In slow $\frac{4}{4}$, beating 8 quavers rather than 4 crotchets.
- With a one-in-a-bar waltz, start with a fast 3 for a few bars until the speed is clarified, before going into 1 (this can also apply to the 'count in').
- In any situation where the music slows down, beat whatever is most useful to clarify the tempo at that point.
- In rock or funk, beat the half beat syncopations if it helps the players.

And that last phrase is key: *if it helps.* You will soon discover whether a subdivision works at a particular point or not.

How do I maintain contact with my performers?
However you go about it – eyes, body language, gestures – your priority must always be to ensure maximum contact with the people in front of you. There is little point in your requesting them to watch you unless you are watching them at the same time. As always this comes back to how well you know the score, not necessarily from memory, but you should not be reading it either. Treat the musical score/lead sheet, in performance at least, as an *aide-mémoire*, something to which you can refer, but not all the time.

A useful analogy is the difference between using an autocue or a set of cue cards for public speaking. Aim to treat the score as the latter.

How might I approach directing from another instrument?
This is not as odd a question as it sounds. Until the mid-18th century there were no official conductors to speak of anyway – but it does require nerve and practice. Whether it be from the keyboard, lead violin or front row saxophone, the key to this sort of leadership is not worrying about being conspicuous, and being happy to make strong, clear gestures; directing from an instrument is not for the self-conscious. You will find yourself doing lots of overt leaning and head nodding, and there will be occasions such as endings or tempo changes where you may have to stop playing altogether for a bar or two.

But this doesn't affect me – I always conduct from the front.
Maybe, but what happens when one of your players is absent at short notice? Would you rather play the crucial keyboard part yourself or get in someone else to do it who has never attended a rehearsal and doesn't even know the music? It happens, and you (and your group) must always be ready for it. This scenario can be practised in rehearsal, of course, putting the onus on your section leaders to take more responsibility for the tempo changes, and it can never do any harm.

Conducting is about much more than beating time correctly, although that does matter. But what matters much more is your ability – through various means – to convey to your performers what you want to happen in the music in the most efficient and convincing way possible. This will only come through rehearsing with real players. Beating time in front of a mirror is fine when you are learning the music, but it is not until you are directing musicians that you will discover whether what you are doing is working or not.

AL CHORAL STYLES ARRANGING
LANNING VENUE VOCALS DYNAMICS
CONDUCTING ADMINISTRATION
Y VENUE SOUND DYNAMICS MANAGING
UP TEACHING CONDUCTING LIGHTING
FORMANCE PRACTICALITIES
CTING SCORING TEACH
VENUE DYNAMICS MANAGING CHORAL
ERCUSSION INS
P LIGHTING SCORING STYLES

CASE STUDY: GILLIAN DIBDEN, TAPLOW YOUTH CHOIR

www.taplowchoirs.org.uk

Who are you?
Gillian Dibden MBE (for services to Youth Choral Music). I was former Head of Voice and Choral Music for the Berkshire Young Musicians Trust. During my time the Berkshire Youth Choir won numerous awards, and was twice named Youth Choir of the Year in the Sainsbury's Choir of the Year competition, winning the overall choir award on one occasion. I was honoured to be named national Choral Director of the Year in 2002. In 2004 I set up Taplow Choirs, and just four years later the Youth Choir won its section in the BBC Radio 3 Choir of the Year competition. The choir has since visited Amsterdam, Estonia and Catalonia, and was invited to take part in a performance of *Elijah* with the Gabrieli Consort and players at the BBC Proms in 2011. I am a mentor for the National Festival of Music for Youth, and also Academic Executive for the Montgomery Holloway Trust.

What is the ensemble?
A mixed SATB Youth Choir for ages 15–18.

IN THE BEGINNING

Who did you expect your audience to be?
Mainly parents, but we also hoped to share concerts with other organisations and charities to raise our profile.

Why did you want to do it?
Mostly parental demand – they felt there was a need for such a choir in the area.

What is/was your unique selling point?
Not only are we the only such choir in the locality, but we give the young people

the opportunity to explore advanced repertoire and to perform in concerts and on tour.

What were your criteria for success?
The priority was always to produce a high standard of music making, combined with a strong social element.

Advertising: how did you do it?
Initially we spent money on a website, flyers, posters and even press adverts. After the first year we scaled this down.

THE ONGOING PROCESS

Do you audition?
Yes, we do audition, although I am always looking for potential more than anything else. Commitment is also key.

For those who are not successful, I always offer advice as to what they need to work on and where they might find help. This is very important.

Venue: how and why did you choose it?
Taplow Village Hall is a logical, central location. It has a good acoustic, although not *too* good – it is always better to go to a concert venue and discover you sound better there than in rehearsal.

Practice times: when, and for how long?
We meet fortnightly on Saturday afternoons for two and a half hours. This has proved to be a very successful strategy, allowing children and parents to plan ahead.

Funding: what system do you have?
We have termly subscriptions covering everything, including aspects such as the cost of music purchase/hire and choir uniform.

Do you have any assistants at rehearsals?
I usually have a pianist who doubles as a male vocal coach when we split into sectionals.

What about administration?
When we started I did all this myself, but as the choir expanded it became impractical so I now employ a part-time PA.

To what extent has your original plan changed?
In essence it has developed naturally, although we could never have envisaged such success, such as the choir being invited to take part in *Elijah* at the BBC Proms in 2011.

What difficulties have you encountered?
- Male recruitment – strong young tenors and basses are hard to find, and I take every opportunity to hear anyone who might be interested.
- Lack of communication regarding absence. We all understand that it happens – there will inevitably be clashes/family issues – but it is helpful if I am informed in advance.

What advice would you give to someone else considering a similar venture?
- Try to be understanding about levels of commitment – most are doing their best. Also, make sure the children have various ways of contacting you, email/mobile and so on.
- Aim to maintain variety in your repertoire, but be wary of purchasing books containing collections/anthologies: you may end up doing very few of the pieces in them.
- Guard against being too cautious with regards to organising concerts and so on. When we started we booked a prestigious concert venue and a tour before we had a choir in place. It focuses the mind and gives everyone something to aim for.

What three key tips can you pass on about organising choral rehearsals?
- Always start on time, no matter how many players are there, and establish that the warm-up is the beginning of the real rehearsal.
- Plan the content of your practices, and always maintain the pace and variety.
- Always remember it is 'their' choir, not yours.

And a tip for performances?
Maintain eye contact with your singers as much as possible – that is where your inspiration comes from.

Who are your musical heroes?
NYC's Michael Brewer, David Hill, Harry Christophers, Gwyn Arch, and the late Ken Weller, former director of the Slough Philharmonic Choir, from whom I learned a great deal. Also the many music teachers across the UK who continue to maintain such high standards with their school choirs – I admire them greatly.

Selecting the music for your group is arguably the most important aspect of leading a musical ensemble. Get it right and the members will love you; get it wrong and they may not even show up. With that level of responsibility on your shoulders, it is crucial that you take it seriously.

What makes it tougher is that there are no right or wrong answers. No book can tell you what music to do with your choir/band/orchestra – it is just something you will have to find out for yourself, and it comes with experience. Every group is different, and may even vary from year to year in what they like doing, so you just have to develop your instinct.

What follows will help to guide you in the early stages.

AIM FOR VARIETY

This is important, not just for your audiences but also for your performers and yourself. With so much music available, you should never need to programme similar pieces all the time, and certainly not in the same concert. Some guidelines:

- **Tempi:** aim for a mix of fast, medium and slow music.
- **Mood:** try to avoid everything being relentlessly upbeat and rousing – it gets wearing after a while. Add some contrasting downbeat and melancholy repertoire.
- **Length:** by all means perform a substantial, ten-minute piece, but look to follow/precede it with something much shorter and lighter.
- **Style:** mix it up if you can. With a pop choir you might do something rocky, followed by a ballad, and then some musical theatre.
- **Key:** even the least musical member of your audience will begin to sense that everything is starting and stopping on the same note/chord, so try to pick pieces in different keys.
- **Solo v small group v ensemble:** it is always nice to contrast features for solo players with full ensemble works. There is also scope for 'splinter groups' from inside the main ensemble – a wind quintet perhaps, or a jazz piano trio in the midst of a big-band concert. With instrumental

groups there is also a practical element to this approach, as it enables other players to have some respite.

- **Actions/movement:** not for every piece, of course, but consider trying something, even if it is just rearranging your choir on stage for the next song. Movement is especially important for younger age groups – junior choirs can clap/stamp/click, and junior bands can stand up/ sit down for various sections of a piece. Always consider the visual element when choosing repertoire for young people.

DON'T BE TOO CAUTIOUS

Many people will tell you that it is always better to play something easy well than to play something challenging badly. While there is undoubted logic in this, it is not always advisable, especially in a mixed-ability ensemble. If you want to hold on to your best players (see Chapter 6) you will need to motivate them, so presenting them with easy, instantly sight-readable parts is not the answer.

This does not mean that everything has to be virtuosic, merely that you should deliberately choose music that will require varying lengths of time to reach performance standard. One piece could be ready after a couple of decent rehearsals, whereas another might take six months to get right.

You also need to be a little wary of your own comfort zone (just choosing music you know and like). That is actually much harder to do than it sounds, but at least be open to ideas from other group members and make sure you listen to their suggestions before making judgements. In the end you ought to be making decisions based on what is right for the group, not just for you, but bear in mind that you will have to teach it to them over a period of time.

KEEP EVERYONE INTERESTED

Aim to find a variety of music which showcases different sections of your ensemble. This is especially true of instrumental groups – the lower brass may not mind the occasional oompah moment, but they will be aggrieved if that is all they get. Similarly, the percussionists may accept one piece for timpani only, but not a whole programme – what is the point in their turning up week after week? Once again, it is about trying to see the process from their point of view, not just your own.

AIM TO DO 'GOOD' MUSIC

There are numerous examples of compositions and arrangements, particularly those written for youngsters, which are very playable but not actually very good. The parts may be strategically written so nobody gets anything too challenging to do, resulting in a confident and convincing performance, but the music itself is bland and uninspiring. Sadly this sort of music often includes inexplicable harmonic simplification, where 'safe' triads are overwhelmingly preferred to 'risky' sevenths and ninths, and dissonance is conspicuously absent.

This can often be true of some lyrics as well, especially educational, worthy ones. Topics such as global warming and bullying do not always lend themselves to imaginative wordplay, so be wary. Your choice may well tick a box with a head teacher or county music advisor, but you may soon find there is nobody in the choir there to learn it.

That is not to suggest that there are not excellent examples of well-written and musically strong music for youngsters/amateurs; there are, but it is your job to find them.

EXPLORE CONTEMPORARY MUSIC

As the group's director it is your responsibility to ensure that you are aware of new developments in your chosen musical style. A pop or gospel choir director should be constantly listening out for new songs, be they the latest hits or other popular songs which might lend themselves to a gospel treatment (see Parts IV and V).

Similarly a brass band conductor should know what the latest 3rd/4th section band test pieces are for the local or national championships. Regardless of whether the group has entered the competition or not, the music should still be worth a look. And wind band directors should aim to keep up with the latest piece by recognised wind band composers – might it work for your band?

DON'T NEGLECT THE CLASSICS

Keeping up to date with the latest music is all very well, but it should not be at the expense of the classic repertoire. This is not just about playing well-known tunes but is much more concerned with learning to perform in certain styles and encouraging a sense of history. Thus, whether in original versions or decent arrangements, the following should be seen as essential repertoire:

- **Orchestras:** Classical symphonies (even if it is only a movement such as a minuet and trio) and possibly some Romantic repertoire. You might also explore the extensive amount of orchestral film music available.

- **Classical/church choirs:** Renaissance polyphony, movements from Baroque oratorios and passions, classical masses and requiems, 19th-century anthems and choral evensongs.
- **Pop choirs:** Motown, The Beach Boys, Simon & Garfunkel, The Beatles, Abba and Queen.
- **Wind bands:** Sousa marches, military music, film scores and Broadway shows.
- **Brass bands:** hymn tunes and traditional marches.
- **Big bands/jazz orchestras:** 1930s/1940s swing music – Ellington, Basie, Goodman, Miller.

Not only is this excellent training, it is also likely to be new music to many of your members, especially younger ones, in which case, encourage them to go away and listen to it before the next practice.

A warning about film music: avoid performing anything other than the main themes/titles, as incidental music/underscoring rarely works without the images and can be dull to listen to and to play. There are exceptions, of course, but not many.

FINDING THE RIGHT REPERTOIRE

Now that you have a good idea of what you are trying to do, how should you go about it? There are several stages.

Listen to demo CDs and online recordings

With so much available on the internet, frequently with accompanying recordings, there is no longer any excuse for the director when it comes to choosing repertoire. Listen to as much as possible and try to aurally superimpose your group's likely performance standards onto the professional rendition you are hearing. Will this piece really work for your group, or are you fooling yourself? Resist the temptation to purchase something purely because you like the arrangement: after attempting it with your members you may grow to hate it just a few weeks later.

Talk to other leaders and take their advice

This is a great way to pick up and share ideas. Of course, you should be wary of taking on similar repertoire to another local group – not only has your unique selling point gone, but there is also the danger of comparison and unnecessary rivalry. However, at this stage you are just exploring ideas and conversation may result in a recommendation for a publisher, a website or even a specific composer.

Attend concerts, festivals and conferences

One of the best ways to discover new repertoire is to hear it performed live, and there are plenty of opportunities to do so. A little research will lead you to a variety of events where you will not only have the chance to hear a range of music done well but may also be able to talk to fellow conductors. In the case of the bigger events there should also be ample opportunity to discuss repertoire with the sales reps on the numerous trade stands in the foyer, and – perhaps the biggest bonus – a chance to study the full scores of many of the pieces to see whether they will work for your group.

Buying music

Once you have decided on the music you want, there are numerous routes you can choose in order to buy it:

- Independent music retailers
- Online sellers, either generalised or specific to sheet music
- Direct from the publisher
- Catalogues and brochures.

Aim to develop a good relationship with your local music shop and you may well find you are given the chance to look at music before you buy it – an ideal scenario.

Hiring music

This is not usually the best option in the long term, as you will want your group to build up a decent and varied repertoire over time, something that cannot happen if the music has to be returned the day after the performance.

However, it can be a good way of getting started, and is also a smart way of dealing with one-off events: your group might be asked to perform something obscure for a wedding, for example, a piece you are happy to do once but which does not fit your standard repertoire.

Borrowing music

Before spending money you do not have, consider the possibility of exploring other sources: local music centres and schools are a good place to start. You can also enquire about inter-library loans, a service that many county libraries offer and in which some specialise.

Arranging music yourself

Providing the piece you wish to do is in the public domain, or you have sought permission from the publisher, doing your own arrangement for your group is often a good way forward. Parts IV and V of this book will guide you through the basics of arranging and should prove a useful resource.

While choosing repertoire is perhaps the most intimidating part of the group leader's role, it is also the most rewarding and exciting. Any musical group that revisits the same pieces year after year will soon stagnate. Aim to do at least one new piece every time you appear in public and, as you become more experienced and the members grow in confidence, you might even attempt the 'no repeat' target – at least for short programmes – where you never perform the same piece in the space of a year.

Your constant search for new (and old) music will lead you to some inspiring discoveries and hitherto unheard composers, no matter how experienced you are as a musician. Attendance at concerts and festivals may yield unexpected contacts and additional performance opportunities, and you are bound to come away with new ideas. And then you will have the thrill of introducing this new music to your players and singers.

PHOTOCOPYING AND COPYRIGHT

While there is no harm in purchasing several one-off copies of a variety of sheet music – usually a choral arrangement – to check on its suitability for your group, it is *totally unacceptable* not to mention *illegal* to then photocopy that music 20+ times for your choir, even if you are not intending to use it in performance. Spare a thought for the professional arrangers – many of whom are paid through the number of copies they sell – and always buy the right number of copies for your group.

TAL CHORAL STYLES ARRANGING
PLANNING VENUE VOCALS DYNAMICS
G CONDUCTING ADMINISTRATION
TY VENUE SOUND DYNAMICS MANAGING
–UP TEACHING CONDUCTING LIG
RFORMANCE PRACTICALITIES
UCTING SCORING TEACHING VE
Y VENUE DYNAMICS MANAGING CHORAL
PERCUSSION CHILTERN CONCERT BAND
IP LIGHTING SCORING STYLES

CASE STUDY: JOHN DAVIE, CHILTERN CONCERT BAND

Founder: John Davie
Conductor: Chris I'Anson
www.chilternconcertband.org.uk

Who are you?
John Davie (LRAM, ARCM, FTCL).
Following a musical career in the Royal
Air Force, including four years as Head of
Woodwind at the RAF School of Music,
I was delighted to become a member of
the team at High Wycombe Music Centre,
holding the post of Woodwind Team Leader
at my retirement in 1998. In addition to
the Chiltern Concert Band I founded the
Bucks Symphonic Wind Ensemble (1987) and the Bucks Youth Wind Orchestra
(1997). I am also still closely involved with the Salvation Army Symphonic Wind
Ensemble. Rather than conducting myself, I have always preferred to find other
musical directors for my bands. I also believe in giving opportunities to up-and-
coming conductors.

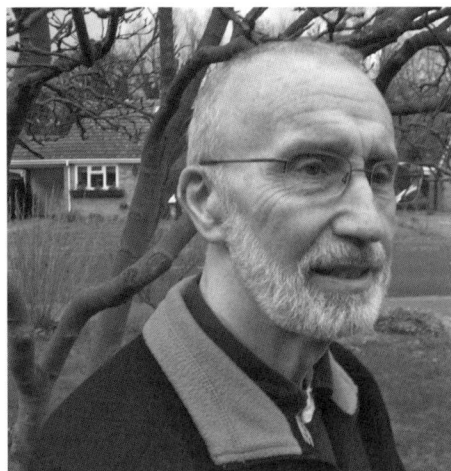

What is the ensemble?
The Chiltern Concert Band (formed 1982): approximately 30 players, aged 17–70.

IN THE BEGINNING

Who did you expect your audience to be?
Anyone who might be interested in listening to us. We also hoped to share
concerts with other groups.

Why did you want to do it?
Necessity really: there were many former members of High Wycombe Music
Centre who had returned from university and had nowhere to play.

What is/was your unique selling point?

High standards, challenging, decent repertoire, and top-class musical direction.

What were your criteria for success? Did you have a one-year/five-year plan?

No, there was never a plan – we would just see how it went. We still are!

Advertising: how did you do it?

For the most part we did not do any advertising, relying instead on player contacts and word of mouth.

THE ONGOING PROCESS

Do you audition?

No, there are no auditions, although we do invite certain players to join us.

Venue: how and why did you choose it?

Equipment storage – mostly percussion – is essential. In our time we have used different venues, including the local music centre and college.

Funding: what system do you have?

All members pay termly subscriptions, or yearly at a discount, with reduced rates for senior citizens. Students (school/college) come for free.

What about administration?

We have a committee, and a music librarian.

To what extent has your original plan changed?

As we did not have an original plan, not a great deal! The fact that the band still exists after 30 years, and is still making good music, is what matters.

What advice would you give to someone else considering a similar venture?

- You must be passionate, dedicated and driven to make it work – it is very much your baby.
- Be willing to keep learning. Attend as many concerts, festivals and conferences as you can, watch the conductors, and discover new repertoire.
- If possible, enable your players to work with a variety of conductors over time – they will learn from it, and so will you.

What three key tips can you pass on about organising ensemble rehearsals?

- Advance planning: you must always know what you are aiming to cover at each practice, and how long you expect each segment to take.

- Know when to stop: if a particular passage is not working well that night, move on to something else.
- Think of the percussion section: if possible, let the players know in advance what order you will do things on that night so they can prepare.

And in performance?
- Know the score – there is no excuse for not doing so.
- Eye contact with your players is key.
- Use your personality to influence what is happening live, and be prepared to take a few risks.

Who are your musical heroes?
Wing Commander (retired) Rob Wiffin, now Professor of Conducting at the Royal Military School of Music, Kneller Hall; Andrew Mackereth (conductor SASWE); Wing Commander (retired) and composer Barry Hingley; Len Wall, violinist; and Jack Brymer, clarinettist supreme.

PART III:
REHEARSING AND PERFORMING

So what should you do when you are faced with a new group for the first time? The members will be experiencing a variety of simultaneous emotions: excitement, fear, nerves, curiosity, a lack of confidence, a sense of 'what am I doing here?'. Pick an emotion and someone in the room will be going through it, including you. Your role is to put them at their ease and help them to make music as soon as possible. Here are a few pointers for a successful first rehearsal.

KNOW THE MUSIC WELL

This is not just about knowing how it goes, but other vital aspects: the mood, feel, structure, style – all of this has to be conveyed to the players, and fast. Make sure you have prepared properly in your own time, with and without the score.

KNOW THE WORDS AND THEIR MEANING

This is not just for choral music but also for instrumental arrangements of songs. How can you presume to teach your band a medley from *Fiddler on the Roof* or *South Pacific* without knowing the lyrics and meaning of the songs? These melodies not only have associated words but contexts (where they fit into the narrative of the story) as well. How else will you be able to explain what the music is trying to convey to the listener?

The same is true of film music: what is the film about, and where does this music appear in it? Some examples:

- The music for *E.T.*: the score by John Williams may conjure up indelible images of airborne bicycles for you, but what if some of your players have never seen it?
- 'One Hand, One Heart' from *West Side Story*: it is easier to create the religious feel if you know that the song portrays a mock wedding.
- 'The Rhythm of Life' from *Sweet Charity*: not a pretty, bouncy song at all, but the compulsive cry of a cult American preacher to his captive and adoring congregation.

As part of an instrumental medley none of the above songs will have lyrics attached, and yet they all have a story to tell. As the musical director, it is your job to tell each short story as effectively as you can in the time available. A little bit of research is all it takes, and it gives you confidence and credibility.

VOCAL WARM-UPS

This is important, but don't get obsessed with it, and don't take too long either. Most professional choral directors will recommend a proper 10/15-minute warm-up, but that is in the *context of a two-hour rehearsal*, so don't overdo it. However, just as dancers and athletes must warm up to prevent pulled muscles, it is important to ensure that your singers' vocal chords are relaxed and working, so do some humming and a few scales at the very least – you don't want everyone going home with a sore throat after your first session, and regular warm-ups will lead to a significant improvement in the quality of the vocal sound.

See the reference section on page 170 for a list of useful books on vocal warm-ups.

INSTRUMENTAL TUNING

There are at least two schools of thought, usually linked to the type of instrumentation in your ensemble, and both have their merits:

A. Tune before starting to play.
B. Play for a bit, then tune once the instruments are warmed up.

1. Orchestras or any other string-based group

These groups always tune in advance because all stringed instruments must be tuned before playing.

What instrument should I tune to?
Clearly this depends on which instruments you have in front of you in the first place, but the principle is based on tuning to an instrument that cannot easily retune itself, or one that is clearly audible while tuning is occurring.

Thus your first option will always be the piano if there is one involved in the piece, as its notes are fixed. In the absence of a piano the standard choice is the oboe, which will be requested to play an A (six notes above middle C). All the other instruments will tune to this note, either all together or in orchestral sections. This is fine for the concert instruments (those in C) – the strings all have an open string to work from – but some of the other instruments not in concert[†] will need to produce other notes to match up to the oboe's A. So, when the oboe/piano plays an A[‡]:

- B♭ instruments (clarinets and trumpets) play a B (a tone higher)
- F instruments (French horns) play an E (a perfect 5th higher)
- E♭ instruments (alto and baritone saxophones) play an F♯ (a major 6th higher).

What should I listen for when tuning?
Once everyone is playing the same note it should be exactly that – the same note. Nobody should be sharp or flat and, in a perfect world, every A will be identical. Don't get too obsessed at this level or you could spend 15 minutes tuning beginners without much success, but it is important that you make everyone aware at this early stage of what they are aiming to achieve and the importance of listening to each other so that they will become used to the process and understand why it matters.

Whose job is it to tell whether someone is in tune or not?
It is yours. As the leader of the group you will be expected to tell every individual whether or not they are in tune, and what to do about it. This is quite a responsibility, and it very much relies on your having a good ear (possessing the ability to spot whether an instrument is in tune or not). As an experienced and successful musician this should be a formality for you by now, but if you are in any doubt about your capabilities in this area, find a 'tame' instrumentalist and practise. It will be well worth it: as with much of the director's role, there is nowhere to hide.

Bear in mind that you are not criticising anyone or commenting on their abilities as a player so don't be afraid to tell individuals they are out of tune in front of the group. There are numerous reasons an instrument might go out of tune, a change in temperature being the obvious one. A flute stuck in a car boot for several hours on a hot day is unlikely to be in tune when first played in an air-conditioned rehearsal room. This is circumstance, not fault, but it still needs to be dealt with. (Having said this, it is amazing how people who practise daily find their instruments to be more reliably in tune than the occasional 'blowers'.)

---

† There are all sorts of practical and historical reasons why these other instruments do not sound the same notes as others, but it is much simpler just to learn what notes to request without explanation. There are also various other instruments in unorthodox keys – trumpets in D, clarinets in A – but at this level you are unlikely to encounter them very often and, if you do, the player will almost certainly know what to do.
‡ This is the conventional approach, although with very inexperienced players you may prefer to tune to concert B♭ for the B♭ and E♭ instruments: but definitely not for strings.

What shall I do if an instrument is out of tune, and how can I solve it?
If you are lucky the players will know what to do themselves, or will be sitting alongside someone who does. However, this will not always be the case, especially with youngsters, so follow this general rule, at least for wind and brass players:

- If too flat, push in; if too sharp, pull out.

This works on the general principle that a longer pipe produces a deeper pitch than a shorter one, we are aiming to lengthen or shorten the tubing to arrive at the right note. The instrument – flute/clarinet/bassoon/saxophone – will consist of sections pushed together, so a slight adjustment at the nearest connection to the mouthpiece will usually pay dividends.

For string players, tiny adjustments should be made with the tuner screws, whereas more extreme problems will require use of the tuning pegs.

As a further check, you may want to find the first block chord of where you are intending to start the piece (not necessarily the beginning – see Chapter 6) and see what it sounds like. You'll soon know if something is amiss.

2. Jazz orchestras

Assuming the group can already play something, no matter how simple, it is quite common for jazz directors to run through a number before tuning officially. This gives all the players a chance to get some air into their instruments and to quite literally warm up. It does not need to be a whole number, just a sufficient amount to give everyone a chance to play. If this is the first rehearsal, just find a starting point in your first piece and get them to play something.

When you do tune, usually to the piano, an A is not much use to the majority of the brass instruments so go for a B♭ on the piano instead. B♭ trumpets will play a written C and trombones (being at concert pitch) play B♭. Then request an A from the piano, allowing the saxes and rhythm section to tune separately (see previous page for the required pitches).

However, having planned to officially tune five minutes in, do encourage everyone to listen to themselves whilst they are playing and adjust accordingly. There is no excuse for still being painfully sharp after playing through a whole piece, and you need to make your expectations clear that the subsequent, official tune-up should really only confirm the fact that everyone is now in tune.

3. Wind bands

Depending on the belief and background of the director, either approach is acceptable. A classically trained leader will opt for the orchestral approach, whereas a leader from a jazz background will probably encourage a bit of playing first.

However, it is always important to tune at some early stage of every instrumental rehearsal and there is no excuse for not doing so. This is especially important with amateurs as it gets them into good musical habits. It also results in your group making a much more pleasing sound.

THE REHEARSAL

Try to get through the piece, or at least most of it

This will depend on the sight-reading abilities of your performers but, if at all possible, try to get through a significant amount of the piece/movement by the end of the first practice (unless it is a symphony, of course!). There are plenty of ways to make this happen, notably with repeated sections. Work through the first appearance of the theme, then jump to its reappearance at the end – it is all about knowing in advance how the piece is constructed. This can be very effective as it boosts everyone's confidence as they realise how much they have covered so soon. Having said this, avoid getting bogged down in tricky (often contrapuntal) sections – skip them and leave them for another time.

Avoid putting pressure on people

Be careful not to focus too heavily on an individual or section; they are unlikely to thank you for it. At this stage avoid exposed passages, although you may like to point them out as key moments in the piece for future practices. At the very least encourage as many players as possible to play the solo line at the start, making it clear that it never does any harm for more than one person to know it.

Don't worry too much about detail

Try to get the gist of the music, and possibly the style. As discussed in Chapter 6, dynamics and phrasing will not normally come until people feel they know the notes. If you wish, focus on a short sequence to demonstrate the importance of detail – starting and ending together, for example – but do not attempt to extend this to the whole piece at this stage.

With more advanced players your strategy may be slightly different, and you should expect dynamic contrasts and articulations to be performed at sight.

Let singers sing the tune

For the first run-through at least, encourage everyone to sing the tune, especially if they already know it. The written harmony parts can come later.

Flag up what you will be doing next week and in the future

Mention some other repertoire you are considering, and a possible event where you are hoping to perform with the group in the future.

The first rehearsal with your group is vital, if only for the fact that you are sending numerous messages to your players during this time. A successful opening practice should:

- Convince the players that you know what you are doing and that you are the person to lead them.
- Assure them that there are plenty of people around them who have the potential to make a decent sound.
- Make it clear that you are passionate about this group and really want it to be a success.
- Emphasise that although you will take it seriously and expect people to practise there will be a lot of fun along the way.
- Persuade the strong musicians to stay, or at least give you a chance for a few sessions before making a decision; this group might have some real potential and they won't want to miss out.
- Encourage as many as possible to come to the next session.

A tall order certainly, but surprisingly possible provided you have done your homework and really believe in what you are doing.

In the next chapter we will consider the ongoing rehearsal sequence.

CHORAL STYLES ARRANGING
LANNING VENUE VOCALS DYNAMICS
CONDUCTING ADMINISTRATION
Y VENUE SOUND DYNAMICS MANAGING
JP TEACHING CONDUCTING
FORMANCE PRACTICALITIES
CTING SCORI A
VENUE DYNAMICS MANAGING CHORAL
ERCUSSION INSTRUMENTAL
P LIGHTING SCORING STYLES

CASE STUDY:
THE COBWEB ORCHESTRA

Administrator: Catherine Shackell;
Creative Director: Andy Jackson
www.cobweborchestra.org.uk

Who are you?
The Cobweb Orchestra started off in County Durham in 1995 as a ten-week course, which was part of a project by Northern Sinfonia outreach worker Andy Jackson and horn player Chris Griffiths. The objective was to encourage lapsed players to brush the cobwebs

Photo: Pauline Holbrook

off their music stands and start playing again. After ten weeks, players were hooked and the orchestra was born, retaining the Cobweb name. The ensemble continued to thrive and, in 2005, management of the orchestra passed to the Sage, Gateshead, although day-to-day running and artistic policy were still under the direction of Andy Jackson.

In 2007 the orchestra became independent. There are currently 250 paid-up members, about 700 players who are involved on a regular basis and 1400 people who follow our activities through e-mail and our website.

The orchestra was the winner of the *Gramophone* Music in the Community Award in 2011.

What is the ensemble?
An orchestra of players of all instruments and abilities that meets in regular, weekly groups and for occasional study days, concerts, residential weekends and foreign trips.

IN THE BEGINNING

Who did you expect your audience to be?
Audience has always been a secondary consideration so we didn't have any specific expectations.

61

Why did you want to do it?
A belief that there were many potential players who would welcome the chance to play music with others, but weren't being offered that opportunity elsewhere.

What is/was your unique selling point?
Genuine open access. Everyone is welcome, old or young, beginner or accomplished player.

What were your criteria for success? Did you have a one-year/five-year plan?
In the beginning success was measured by numbers attending. Now, as an independent organisation, we also have to try to balance the books, so we do now have a five-year plan.

Advertising: how did you do it?
Flyers and posters, followed by a website. More recent media attention all helps to promote what we offer.

THE ONGOING PROCESS

Do you audition?
No.

Venue: how and why did you choose it?
We have changed venue several times since the start due to growth of numbers.

Funding: what system do you have?
Players pay per weekly session with a reduction for membership. We also support the orchestra with regular fundraising events.

What about administration?
We have a part-time creative director, an administrator and volunteers.

To what extent has your original plan changed?
We didn't have a plan at the start, but demand for expansion led to other regional orchestras all over northern England.

What difficulties have you encountered?
- Becoming independent of a large, publicly funded organisation was a major challenge.
- Various musical and interpersonal issues that inevitably arise.

- Managing expectation: maintaining our core ethos (open access) while ensuring a quality experience for all players and, where appropriate, audiences too.
- Developing and maintaining a fit-for-purpose website requires constant attention.

What advice would you give to someone else considering a similar venture?
- Be on top of essential musical skills – score reading, conducting technique, extensive instrument knowledge, composition, arranging, transposition and repertoire.
- Get a good team around you – you can't do everything yourself.
- Never listen to bad advice, but listen to everyone who means well, even if you've heard it hundreds of times before.

What three key tips can you pass on about organising ensemble rehearsals?
- Develop your radar: you need to be aware of everything that's happening in the room before everybody else.
- Prepare meticulously, but don't have a rigid plan. Be prepared to work with the people in the room to achieve the best outcome possible on every occasion. Always focus on the people in front of you.
- Recognise that everybody has strengths and qualities, not necessarily musical. Nurture these qualities rather than emphasise shortcomings.

And tips for performances?
- Talk to audiences about the music you are playing, but don't say too much. Three things to listen out for will be ample.
- Remember that you are the person the audience watches most because you are moving. The music is transmitted to the audience through you. It's a huge responsibility and you need to take this seriously.
- Dress well and appropriately.

Assuming you have picked the right repertoire and delivered a decent first rehearsal, the attendances at practices from now on should be reasonably solid. Now you can start to work with the performers and make some real music. This is the most exciting and creative part of the process, a time when you can try things, safe in the knowledge that nothing is set in stone yet.

Here are three rhetorical questions for you to bear in mind:

1. **What will encourage them to come back next week?** It is not enough to say 'Choir is on a Tuesday, and they have to come', what incentive do they have? If they don't show up for one week, what will they miss out on? This is especially crucial for the strong musicians who form the core of your ensemble – you must keep them interested.

2. **What have they learned in today's rehearsal?** It is no good just repeating what you did last week in the hope that it will get better, you must have an aim for each practice, and all the participants must leave having learned something new.

3. **What do you enjoy/hate when you are being rehearsed by somebody?** This is a useful exercise – whatever drives you mad will probably have the same effect on others, so don't do it to them. Waiting to do something is a major issue – always aim to keep everyone interested and involved in some way, even when doing sectionals.

REHEARSAL DISCIPLINE

Unless you are very fortunate there will inevitably be a tendency to chat among some people. This is by no means confined to youngsters – adults can be just as bad. The level of chatting you allow will depend on the angle you are taking with your group and the level of importance attached to the social element. As discussed in Chapter 1, one of the ways to motivate group members to return week after week is to encourage and nurture potential friendships, especially new ones, which may well continue outside the sessions as well.

There are many reasons why people chat when they should be working: reactions to what is going on; nervousness; sometimes covering up a perceived inability to cope; even discussions about the music itself if you are lucky. Whatever the reason, it is unlikely that they are aiming to be intentionally disruptive, and this is worth remembering. However, you cannot have a rehearsal constantly interrupted by extraneous noise; it will waste valuable time, and may also annoy those who want to get on with things. There are numerous strategies for dealing with this, two of which might be:

- Insert a break, assuming the rehearsal is long enough, of course, and encourage people to mix then. Alternatively, you could finish unexpectedly early on occasions.
- When you want to rehearse, go ahead with the minimum of preamble – 'three, four, in!' – and reprimand, gently at first, anyone who does not come in when they should. People will soon get the message, and you remain in control of the situation.

Not only are there several strategies available but there are also different levels of tolerance. You will know what you can cope with, so that is the level you must set. Circumstances can also dictate levels of chat. It might not be so much of a concern in week three, but a major issue in the penultimate rehearsal before the concert when time is at a premium.

Just remember that, at amateur level at least, the members are there to have a good time and in the end that is why they will come back.

HOLDING THE INTEREST OF THE STRONG PERFORMERS

In many ways this is the most important part of your role: how do you keep good musicians coming back for more when those around them are slower to learn things than they are? You cannot afford to lose these people as they are the core of your group. The key is to ensure they feel important and wanted, you must never take them or their presence for granted.

Some approaches:

- Talk to them about your aspirations for the group and potential next stages. They will be pleased to see some ambition from you.
- From the start, get them involved in the structure of rehearsals. Discuss with them which piece they think you should start with after the break, or which song they feel needs the most work. (Of course you should already know, but it is interesting to see what others are feeling as well.)
- Encourage them to take on roles of minor responsibility, such as basic administration. They may also be interested in organising break refreshments or even a social gathering.
- Always make it clear to them that you know they are strong and that you have high expectations of them.

- If possible, aim to feature these individuals quite early on in the process, perhaps by giving them a solo role. It does not have to be too major, just enough to show that you trust them. The ultimate honour will, of course, be buying or even arranging a piece to feature them as soloists/duets/trios.
- Offer them *secondary leadership roles*. You might invite your top saxophone player to rehearse the wind section in another room, or your experienced soprano to check that all is well with her less confident colleagues. They are unlikely to do much damage and may well develop a sense of camaraderie within these sectionals, something you would have found tricky to do yourself as the 'outsider'.

Throughout all of the above your aim is to make your top musicians feel that this group will not be as good without them, and that their presence really makes a difference. You have appreciated their talents and are constantly showing them that they are important to you as an ally – 'together we can make this work' is your underlying message.

How many pieces should I aim to do per rehearsal?
You should aim to cover several pieces per session, provided you remember the two differing approaches: 'running through' and 'working on'.

RUNNING THROUGH

This might happen at the start or end of a practice, or even just before the break. It needs to be a reasonable chunk of music – at least two minutes – and it does not need to be perfect. In an ideal world it should not stop unless there is no alternative. The run-through serves two key purposes:

- **For the performers**: it reminds everyone how the piece goes and gives them some idea of how well they know it. A full run also gives a sense of shape and length of the piece. This can be useful for brass players, for example, who will discover how much stamina they require, and percussionists might also benefit, especially if they are being required to change instruments mid-piece and need to know how long the gap is between their cymbal crash and imminent xylophone solo.
- **For you**: it informs you of how well learned the piece is at this stage, and how much more rehearsal it will require to reach performance level. You can listen for sections which still need work, some of which may be a surprise, and mentally build in rehearsal time to rectify these problems. A run-through will also highlight sections of the piece which you have so far barely looked at, or even missed altogether. However, on a more positive note, you can hopefully confirm that a significant amount of the piece is reasonably solid at this stage in the rehearsal process.

The most important aspect of the run-through is that it allows everyone to make music together. There are no stops and starts, no pedantic picking out poor dynamic contrasts or ragged ensemble endings – everyone gets to hear and perform the piece as it is meant to be done. This is, after all, why they are there in the first place. It can also be important for irregular attenders/newcomers to find out how the music goes.

So, run-throughs are great and vital for everyone, but remember this important point:

No piece can be improved just by running it through again and again.

Granted, the music might start to develop continuity and a sense of style but, in essence, the performance will be no better the second or third time than it was the first. For that you must switch to the other approach: working on a piece.

WORKING ON

This is the polar opposite of the run-through and it is hard work, although it can be immensely satisfying. This part of the rehearsal involves taking a section of the music – sometimes no more than a few bars – and working at it until it is correct, or at least significantly better than before. The process must be systematic, detailed and disciplined, and you as the leader must not accept second best: if it is not good enough, do it again and again until it is. Choose an aspect to work at such as dynamics, articulation, phrasing, breathing, diction, and stick to it. Do not be tempted to go on until you are reasonably happy with the result – it is counterproductive and you are entering 'run-through' territory, which must be avoided, at least until the end of this section of the practice.

Might people get bored?
Not if they improve, and it is your job to make sure they do and that they can hear the improvement. Once your performers start to realise that the detailed work is paying off and making a difference, everything should be fine.

What about keeping the experienced musicians interested?
The strong, experienced players will expect you to take this approach and are likely to quit if you don't. They, of all the members, will understand that it is the only way to improve the sound of the group and that there are no shortcuts. They should appreciate your efforts and intentions, and it will confirm your ambition for the group and the desire to aspire to new heights. It will take time to achieve those heights, of course, but at least you are going about it the right way. Without this detailed work the group is never likely to rise beyond a basic level and, as a result, your top performers may lose interest.

In conclusion, both 'running through' and 'working on' have their place in every rehearsal, just as they do in any individual instrumentalist's practice session, and you should aim to mix them up. As a general guide:

- Do not plan to run through a piece you are working on
- Do not plan to work on a piece you are running through.

Note the use of the word 'plan' though – it does not always work out that way and each rehearsal is different, with different priorities (see below). However, in general practice it is a good rule to follow.

So, let's assume you have decided to do some work on a piece or a section of it. What aspects might you work on? We will start with general points which can be applied to all ensemble rehearsals, followed by sections focusing on aspects specifically relevant to instrumental or choral groups.

GENERAL REHEARSAL TECHNIQUES

Knowing the notes

As the group leader you will be itching to work on the interesting elements of the music, eager to put across your own ideas of style and genre and all the other nuances that make performing (and rehearsing) such a thrill. However, the details of dynamics/phrasing and so on (see below) are all very well, but not much of that will happen until the performers – especially if they are inexperienced – feel reasonably confident that they know the notes. You must try to see it from their point of view: 'Why are you bothering to tell me how loudly to sing the note at the start of the second line when I haven't got the note itself right yet, and have no idea how to do so?'

Not only should you try to spot potentially awkward areas in the music, but you must also encourage your performers to let you know when they are having difficulty or are simply lost, and tell them that there is no shame in this. It is far better for all concerned if you sort out the late cello entry which is causing the flutes to miss their cue rather than continuing blindly on hoping it will all get better or, even worse, not even acknowledging that there is a problem.

So what's the best way for people to learn their notes?
- **Slow practice:** this is usually the answer (and can be one of the major disadvantages of exclusive use of backing tracks which only ever go at full speed), although do ensure that you confirm how the line should go before sending them off to practise elsewhere in their own time.
- **Repetition:** go over lines/phrases in 'working on' rehearsal segments, and do not be scared to do so – once is not enough. When people get it right, give them the satisfaction of getting it right again before moving on.

- **Individual practice**: where possible, encourage the players to take their music home and work on it, perhaps with their instrumental teachers if they have individual lessons. This is more difficult for singers, particularly if they cannot read music, so consider the possibility of recording the lines for them to sing along to, perhaps in the car on the way to and from work. This is time-consuming for you, but acknowledging the need for it may lead to your being able to take on some more challenging repertoire as a result; it might just be worth the effort. At the very least, if your members can see that you have spent all this time helping them they are much more likely to feel obliged to respond in a positive manner and do their homework.

Outside learning is underrated, and not just from your viewpoint. It is undoubtedly true that any member who has made the effort to prepare will get much more out of the session as a result, and this is even more evident when it comes to performance: the confidence and self-belief will be much higher. The sooner they know the notes, the sooner the real music making can start.

Ensemble: playing together

There are very few styles of music where being together and listening to each other are not essential, so make ensemble a high priority with whatever group you are working with, and never be satisfied with second best.

As always when performing music, the ears are the most important tool – there is no substitute for listening. Most people should be able to tell when things are not together. However, putting it right is not always easy. Some suggestions:

- **Breathing in time for the entry**: not just for singers, but wind and brass players as well. Those players whose instruments only just make it to their lips at the last minute will almost certainly be late in coming in, and that will spoil the overall attack in the section as a whole.
- **Rests**: regard them as being as important as the notes (see 'Silences and rests' on page 76). There is little point in everyone starting at the right time if the end of the note/phrase is ragged.
- **Clapping**: with tricky homorhythmic sections (everyone doing the same) ask people to clap the passage rather than sing/play it. Then, in the case of instrumentalists, you can move on to the next stage.
- **Singing for instrumentalists**: as above, but with voices instead of instruments. In both cases it will soon become clear which part of the phrase is causing the problems (and to whom) and it should be possible to sort it out. When the phrase is eventually played it should be correct.
- **No rhythm section/backing track**: a strong regular rhythm can often cover up a lot of guesswork. See how the group copes without the crutch of a drum beat – is everyone still together and listening to each other?

Lengthy rests/silences can also be revealing. Does everyone come in at the right time after such a gap?

- **No conductor** (see below): the logical conclusion to all of the above. Can everyone breathe together and come in correctly without your help? Encourage them to listen harder and to sense the ensemble around them.

Multi-part training

With your strong performers it is a good idea to get them to learn as many parts as possible, assuming it is within their ranges. This will enable them to assist other sections during rehearsals and give confidence to those players/ singers who find themselves on their own for a weekly session. For instance:

- Trombonists might assist with the bassoon, cello or tuba part.
- Second sopranos might learn both the first soprano and alto lines.
- Altos might learn the tenor line.
- First violins might switch between their part and that of the second violins.
- Linked to the above, you might ask the first clarinets or flutes to assist the seconds or thirds at an exposed or contrapuntal entry before rejoining their own line once everything is up and running. Composers and arrangers do not always consider this aspect in their writing, perhaps assuming that all players are as good as each other. This is rarely the case at junior or amateur level, so you may need to take this into account if at all possible. Anyone – from any section if necessary – who is available to 'launch' an entry should be called upon to do so, at least in rehearsal.

Very experienced players might even be persuaded to transpose another part – a top alto sax player could learn the French horn line or vice versa. This is tricky, but it will certainly keep your strong players on their toes and prevent boredom.

There is another reason for the above. If by any chance anyone is ill or unavailable for the performance, especially at short notice, you may have no alternative but to ask someone to cover another part on the day. An SATB choir arrangement is unlikely to work harmonically without a tenor line, so a capable low alto will need to step in, possibly assisted by a light baritone if he can be spared from the bass section. It is much better for them if they have had a chance to at least look at the other parts in advance. Your role as director is to make sure that all of the most important entries happen somehow, and that all the chords and textures are as complete as possible in performance.

This sort of advance planning frequently pays off, and if the strong players get used to their multipurpose roles they will become increasingly confident and even look forward to the challenge – yet another way of keeping them interested.

Technical skills

As the leader you will be regarded as the fount of all knowledge, and some of your members will expect you to answer all their questions about their instruments. Unless you are a multi-instrumentalist it is wise to set some ground rules for yourself at the start:

1. If someone wants to know the bassoon fingering for high A♭, gently explain that you are not a bassoonist and suggest playing the note down the octave for the time being (or you could check the score and offer an alternative note that would fit the harmony just as effectively). The key message to convey is that the player shouldn't worry about it today but try to find out the answer by the next rehearsal.
2. You will definitely be expected to comment on your areas of strength. Thus, if you are a string player, you should demonstrate your specialist knowledge as a matter of course and help your players to improve with tips and tricks of the trade. It will look odd if you don't and could undermine your credibility, so don't be shy.
3. You might consider learning a little more about the instruments/voices you are working with. Purchase some fingering charts perhaps, or if you are running a choir but have never had singing lessons consider taking some, making it clear to your teacher that you are looking for tips and techniques you can pass on to others. The more you begin to understand the problems your singers and players are encountering, and how to deal with them, the more effective a director you will become.

Dynamics

Anything you can do to make your group sound more interesting is a worthwhile exercise, and dynamics are a key part of this. This is not simply about louds and softs, but the *reasons* behind them.

How can my group get better at dynamic contrast?
Most groups can instantly do basic loud and soft, but it is *how loud and how soft* that matters. The expectations must always come from you, and you must never be too easily satisfied, especially at the quiet end; it is almost always possible to play/sing quieter and still be heard. Aim to emphasise the importance of *extremes* from a very early stage. The key is the word 'contrast', a difference which must be clearly audible to the audience as well as the performers. Be wary of high volume levels – these can lead to a brash,

unpalatable noise from the brass and high wind players – but make sure your performers are not afraid to be loud when it is required.

Composers and arrangers of popular music are not always helpful with this. All too frequently you will be given minimal information as to the ideal dynamic level. However, this does not mean that there are no dynamics; you just need to devise them yourself.

Inexperienced instrumental players and dynamics

Be aware that, although your players may understand and want to do all the dynamics you ask from them, they may not yet be technically capable of producing the range of contrast you are requesting. Inexperienced wind and brass players in particular will suffer from this problem as they go through the process of learning breathing technique and developing their stamina. They simply cannot play quietly for fear of the fact that the instrument will not speak at the right time. Be sympathetic to their situation, praising any contrasts you hear while also stressing the importance of dynamic range. It will come eventually.

Singers have much less excuse. If your choir fails to sing quietly, get them to whisper instead to prove they can do it. Inexperience will lead to some breathing issues, especially in longer phrases, and this might affect the sound, but on the whole it should be possible to get a choir to sing very quietly from a very early stage in the rehearsal process. Perhaps surprisingly it is actually harder for inexperienced singers to produce loud sounds, as this requires much more confidence and also a lot more technique. Bear that in mind when you are asking them for more volume at the end of a big number – they will be doing their best.

Balance

This is strongly linked with dynamics, but in this case different sections have different dynamic levels at the same time. The key to balance is to identify the most important musical line at any given moment.

- Who has the tune? Your audience will want to hear it, and will be frustrated if they cannot.
- Who has the accompaniment? A long line of semibreves is unlikely to be the melody, so train your members to spot this and react accordingly.
- Who is providing the bass line/rhythm? This is the engine room of the group: crucial, but rarely noticed if done convincingly.

This is basic, though important, stuff, but it can be much more complex than this and it is part of your role to help your performers to understand the nuances of balance. For example:

- **Changing roles**: it is rare that the same instrument will have the same role (as outlined above) throughout the piece, or even in the same 16-bar phrase. Make sure your performers understand when their roles change, and how. They must also recognise when someone unexpected gets the tune: the tuba perhaps, or bass guitar.
- **New musical ideas**: the tune is not always the most important line, as the ear may become overly familiar with it and switch off. In this case a new idea – a rhythmic backing figure or a contrasting countermelody – might take precedence, so encourage your player/singer to bring the line out from within the texture.
- **Chord balance**: if there are three notes in a chord, which is the most important? Not necessarily the tonic/key note, it could be the major/minor third, or even the seventh/ninth in a jazz-based context. In a series of chords it is usually the *moving parts* that matter – bring them out.
- **The feel and colour**: in popular music, it is the 'feel' (also known as the 'groove') that makes the music work – the specific interacting drum and bass lines that create the sense of reggae/gospel/jazz/disco. But it won't always be just the rhythm section that provides colour, others may have key roles to play as well. A harmonica will help create the essence of the blues, or an accordion might produce a recognisable 'French' ambiance. There is little point in any of this happening (or being written) if it is being drowned out by others.

Blend

This is especially important in a choir, where you are aiming to hear as few individual voices as possible (apart from solos, of course). You will need to train your singers to listen to each other and to keep checking whether their voice is sticking out of the texture or not. Sadly it is not as simple as it sounds. For an inexperienced performer, the most obvious response is to drop the volume and hide inside the section, which is exactly the opposite of what you want to happen. Each voice needs to make an impact, but as part of the overall texture.

At a more sophisticated level you will eventually want to work on aspects such as unified vowel sounds – not everyone's 'O's or 'E's will be the same to start with and the discrepancy will be noticeable. This will become even more important when you are singing with an accent. In an ideal world everyone will have to produce exactly the same vowel sounds for the effect to work.

Blend is also important in an instrumental context, although arguably it is much more linked with balance here. However, the aim is still the same: no individual player should stick out of the texture unless they are meant to do so. The easiest way to work on this is via sections – strings, wind, brass – concentrating on getting the *same sound colour* from each player.

Achieving an effective blend is a never-ending quest for every ensemble, professional just as much as amateur, and it will guarantee considerable improvement of the group over time, if only because your members are being forced to use their ears in rehearsals.

Phrasing and articulation

Whether it is in choral or instrumental music, phrasing matters. Short, chopped-up phrases are very different from long, sweeping lines, and you must always aim to get them right if you are to set the right mood. It is most important to ensure that all members of the group are phrasing the same lines of music in exactly the same way, even if the lines appear in different sections of the piece. Try this:

- Through your own demonstration, which might be playing or singing, make sure everyone understands how you want a particular phrase to work.
- Ask everyone who has (or will have) this specific phrase to practise it together, regardless of where the lines actually appear in the music. This may mean that the sopranos start at bar 10 and the altos start at bar 18 and they sing at the same time (even if the notes are a 5th apart). It all saves time and ensures that everyone phrases the same way. This technique works particularly well in music which is imitative (of which fugue is the most extreme example). Much better for everyone to learn exactly the same musical line together than one part at a time, and much more satisfying for all concerned. Once again, your preparation is key: you must know the exact locations of the various musical lines and be able to communicate that instantly to the group.

Articulations and accents

The above approach can also be applied to articulations and accents. Most sections of the group will play the same music at some point, so find where that is and make them all do it together. If there are accents on notes two and four in a specific phrase, check that everyone is doing it. The cellos may not have that pattern until 52 bars later but, when it arrives, they should know exactly how it is to be played.

All of the above, with everyone involved and playing together, creates a strong sense of teamwork and ensures that nobody feels too embarrassed. The waiting is cut to a minimum, and any potential solo performers – the horn player perhaps, or the one-man tenor section of your choir – do not feel overexposed.

Teaching complex rhythmic patterns

This can be tricky, notably in Latin-American music or jazz funk where the notated rhythms are almost impossible to read at sight. The composer has laboriously written it down in a series of semiquavers, but to no avail: very few of your players can actually read it correctly. And yet it is this very brass figure or bass line (think of the extended brass hook in the middle of Stevie Wonder's 'Sir Duke', for example) that makes the whole piece special.

You have to know it, of course, either by learning it in advance or just listening to a recording if you are lucky, but how do you convey it to your group?

Should we just slow it down?
Breaking down the pattern into semiquavers takes a long time and destroys the rhythmic drive – few of these punchy jazz rhythms sound great at a quarter speed. You may get it right, but everyone will wonder why they are bothering. Try this instead:

- *Clap* the rhythm, reasonably close to the actual tempo, and get them to clap it back to you (several times) until it is right. Do not be afraid to break the line into smaller bits, not necessarily in the order they appear, and put the music together like a jigsaw.
- Ask your group to play/sing the phrase on one note to get the feel and articulation right. Unison is wise, but any note will do as the exercise is purely about rhythm at this point.
- Finally, put the written notes back in. If you have done the previous work properly, the result should be spot on and there will be a great sense of achievement in the room.

Blocks of sound

At the same time, try to get your performers to see groups of notes as *blocks of sound*, not a series of individual notes: 'If you see this two-bar rhythmic phrase it will always sound like this.' In the end this sort of approach becomes automatic and your members will start to spot the same phrases cropping up again and again in numerous pieces.

If you want to perform gospel, jazz funk, or any sort of popular music, you cannot avoid syncopation and complex rhythmic patterns, and neither can the members of your group. However, approached in the right way, allowing the musical drive to do its work, this is not as intimidating and time-consuming as it might appear.

Practising swung quavers

With the possible exception of the classical orchestra, every musical ensemble will have to learn to swing at some stage. This is not the place to explain swing – if indeed it is possible – but, paradoxically, often the best way to rehearse awkward swing passages is to remove the swing altogether and straighten the rhythm into even notes. Approaching the pattern as a rock or Latin-American phrase, perhaps accompanied by the drum kit if available, is usually much easier, as it is clearer where each of the notes fits into the bar/beat. Once all queries have been addressed it should be simple enough to put the swing back in.

Silences and rests

These can be just as important as the notes themselves, and they can take many forms:

- **Total silence:** everybody stops, usually for a dramatic purpose, before continuing.
- **Rests as a group:** everyone has staccato notes, with gaps in between, to create a crisp, bouncy feel.
- **Rests in individual parts:** one instrument stops playing, enabling another to cut through the texture and be clearly heard. Without the carefully structured rest the second instrument's key entry will be lost (see 'Balance' on page 72).
- **Rhythmic rests:** a break just before a syncopated entry, sometimes filled by the drums, allowing the player to mentally bounce off the rest and ensuring that the next entry is spot on (see 'Air drumming' on page 87 for more explanation).

Rehearsing silences

The explanation is simple: if the composer writes a quaver he/she means a quaver – nothing more, nothing less. Similarly, a dotted minim is three beats long, not three-ish.

Be insistent and rarely satisfied. Request the offending phrase to be repeated until everyone is playing the correct length of note. At the same time, make it clear that there is never any excuse for getting the lengths of notes wrong. Of course, you may change the durations of notes for your musical purposes, usually when the composer has neglected to provide any opportunity to breathe, but it will be your decision which you then communicate to the group. Otherwise, train your singers and players to follow what the composer has written as a matter of course.

No matter what the style of music, if you continue to let your group play/sing through rests, or to shorten notes through laziness, that group will never sound any good. Whether it is a band or a choir it will always come across as ragged and half-hearted; the audience may not even know why, but the sense will be there. There will be a lack of clarity – mostly caused by the new musical lines being drowned out by others which should have stopped by now – and that elusive ensemble feel will remain a distant dream. You must be tough on rests and note lengths, even from day one. It will pay off much sooner than you think.

Sectional practices

The opportunity to work in detail with a part of your ensemble should always be incorporated into a rehearsal schedule if at all possible. There are so many advantages, not least of which is the knowledge that nobody is sitting in the corner doing nothing. A sectional enables you to hear what is really going on, and encourages collaboration between yourself and the players as you sort out problems between you. There is also an element of expectation – players who know they have a sectional next week are more likely to practise beforehand, as there will be nowhere to hide. Just remember to make a sectional rehearsal shorter than a standard one, or incorporate more breaks as everyone will be working much more intensively than usual.

However, be wary. Although musically desirable, sectionals can cause unforeseen problems for the group as a whole. For example, it is not always wise to call a strings-only rehearsal for the following week, as the rest of the orchestra will get out of their regular attendance pattern. This is a particular issue with youngsters. In general, aim to have everyone attending at least part of the rehearsal – maybe the first or second half – before splitting up. Even better, depending on the number of rooms to which you have access, devise a scenario where everybody attends the whole rehearsal but splits into separate groups. Not only does this maintain the rehearsal habit, it also enables everyone to reconvene at the end of the session to hear how much improvement has occurred in the meantime.

This last point is much more important than it may seem. For many of your players and singers, the major reason they turn up week after week is to perform with others. They crave the overall teamwork and, in every sense, harmony. You may wish for the luxury of checking the unison trumpet line with a small group of players while everyone else takes an extended coffee break, but this is not what the majority are there for.

Escaping the front

As the group's leader it is likely that most of your rehearsal time will be spent in the same tiny area of the room, positioned right in front of your performers.

This is all too predictable, and not always helpful either, and you should aim to avoid it for at least some of the time. Some potential problems:

- You are always surrounded by exactly the same people in every rehearsal, reinforcing a front row/back row mentality in your players which is not helpful.
- Due to where you are positioned you may find yourself doing much more rehearsal work with those nearest to you. You are more likely to hear their mistakes, and you will certainly talk to them much more than, for example, the distant percussion.
- Anyone at the back who feels like switching off can easily do so, in contrast to the front row performers who are under your nose.

Whenever possible you need to deliberately free yourself from the front desk and move around the space. If you are not convinced the trumpets are concentrating well enough, for example, go and stand behind them; in most cases they will be glad of the help. Once you have sorted out the problem there is no need to return to the front instantly – just count the group in and stay with the trumpets to confirm that all is now well. Standing at the rear or in the middle of any group reminds you how others are actually hearing the music, and it is a very useful experience.

It also raises alertness. If anyone in the room thinks you might come over to see how they are doing at any point in the rehearsal it should sharpen the communal concentration levels.

This approach, which is usually most effective around halfway through the rehearsal sequence when the music is mostly learned but the detail is lacking, keeps everyone (including you) on their collective toes and maintains the required energy levels.

Working without the conductor

Following on from the above, as your members become more confident start to leave them to it. Help them to realise that they don't always need you for every single entry, and encourage some leadership in your sections.

For instrumental groups

- Competent drummers or percussionists do not need someone beating $\frac{4}{4}$ time in front of them – they will be fine. The same applies to other members of the rhythm section. Trust them to do their jobs, allowing you to concentrate on other instruments.

- Force everyone to listen to one another, breathe together, count properly so they come in correctly, taking responsibility for their performance without being spoon-fed from the front.
- See how the group copes with time changes without your help. You'll be surprised how dispensable you prove to be.
- Emphasise to everyone the important role of the front row leader (first violin in an orchestra, probably flute/clarinet/saxophone in a band). A good leader should be able to do almost everything you do, so encourage them to take more responsibility.

For choirs

- **Piano accompaniment:** can your singers cope without it? Can they stay in time, and in tune? This is a useful exercise if you are the only pianist, as it allows you to escape from the keyboard as well as testing out your singers.
- **Backing track:** try not using it, or fading it out at certain points without warning.

In both cases your plan is to remove the safety net. It will be back in performance, of course, but that's several weeks away. The rule is simple: if they can do it without, they can certainly do it with. This sort of unaccompanied/undirected practice develops confidence in your performers and the sense of ownership is greatly enhanced.

Practising without the conductor has many advantages and should be done as much as possible once the music is reasonably solid. Not only does it develop self-belief in your performers, but a group which is used to this experience will not be fazed when you leave them to their own devices at the pre-concert rehearsal to check the acoustics and balance (see Chapter 7).

Talking over the music

Some may disagree, but talking can be useful and certainly much more efficient than stopping to discuss things, especially if practice time is limited. In reality you don't tend to talk over what the performers are doing anyway, it is usually in the space between phrases.

In general your aim is to encourage while also suggesting improvements. Use phrases linked to:

- **Detail:** 'more diction please' or 'not too loud here'.
- **Repeated musical patterns:** 'good, but more punchy next time' or 'let's make the next one quieter'.

- **Timing:** at the apex of long phrases – 'we're aiming for … *this* note!'
- **General encouragement:** 'that's more like it' or 'I knew you could do it!'

Talking over the music energises the whole rehearsal and keeps everyone focused, including you, and there is always something to say. It also means that the music gains a sense of continuity – it can be so frustrating when the conductor stops every two seconds to explain a tiny point, when all they had to do was to allow the performers to improve on their first effort a mere two bars later, where exactly the same phrase is due to appear. Of course, you will have to stop and explain things occasionally but, if possible, treat your rehearsals like a decent sporting referee and *let them flow*; after all, everyone is there to make music, not to listen to you.

LISTENING TO RECORDINGS

If you are fortunate to have access to a recording of the piece you are doing it is certainly a good idea for you to listen to it. It will enable you to get an idea of the shape of the piece as a whole and increase your familiarisation. In an ideal world, you really ought to be approaching the ability to direct much of the piece from memory before you stand in front of your group for the first rehearsal of the work.

However, beware. Assuming it is a professional group you are listening to, always try to factor in how your group will sound when performing this piece as opposed to the Berlin Philharmonic Orchestra, the Central Band of the Royal Air Force or the London Community Gospel Choir. This is especially important when choosing repertoire (see Chapter 4). Ask yourself these questions:

- Will your brass section really be able to 'ring out' like that?
- Are your bass singers genuinely going to be able to attack that choral entry with the level of vigour the music requires?
- Assuming your group won't be able to play the piece as fast as indicated, will the music itself still work at a slower speed or will it just drag? An example might be the final section of the overture to *William Tell*, or perhaps a Gilbert and Sullivan patter song such as 'Modern Major General' – exhilarating at full speed, but very dull at half tempo.

This last point is crucial. Plenty of pieces across all genres have a correct speed – alter that and the effect can be disastrous or just underwhelming. Remember, if music is composed to be fast, it probably needs to go fast to work.

Should we listen to a recording in rehearsal or not?
Clearly you cannot stop your members listening in their own time – singers will frequently want to join in with the recorded version of the piece they are doing, for example, even if it is in a different key. However, communal listening during

a rehearsal must be treated with care as it can be counterproductive at times if not fully explained.

Why? Surely it can only help?
Not necessarily. It can be intimidating for amateurs to hear a professional group perform their piece. 'We'll never be that good' is a natural reaction, and it could be demoralising. The potential for such a reaction may also be evident when a simplified arrangement is involved. The theme to *Star Wars* arranged for amateur wind band will never sound as spectacular as the full John Williams orchestral version, so rehearsing your arrangement can be a bit of a disappointment after such an exhilarating sonic experience just minutes before.

In some ways it might be more useful for your players/singers to hear a version of a similar but different piece – in the above scenario perhaps an arrangement of *Raiders of the Lost Ark*. This will enable you to discuss and highlight the various elements you will need to work on, many of them listed above, but without hearing the actual notes they will be playing. This approach can be particularly effective for big-band swing. Listen to a Benny Goodman or Artie Shaw recording (it does not need to be the actual piece you are working on) and aim to teach good habits and style.

In all cases, draw attention to various points of style and ensemble, such as pointing out the vocal sounds specific to gospel singing, and leave it at that. As long as the result is inspiring rather than depressing you will be fine, but do tread carefully.

FOR INSTRUMENTAL GROUPS ONLY

(Turn to page 86 for choral groups)

The importance of the rhythm section

No instrumental group will function successfully until the rhythm section gets it right. It does not have to be the drummer – it might be a Baroque continuo or the tubas in a brass band – but unless those providing the rhythmic feel (groove) at any given point understand what to do, the rest of us may as well pack up and go home. This may seem harsh, but it is true and needs to be addressed; spend time with the rhythm section and soon everything else will fall into place; ignore the rhythm section and you will waste a lot of time and create a great deal of frustration and anger in the rest of the band, many of whom will recognise where the real problems lie and will wonder why you don't do something about it. It is worth it even if only a section of the piece is affected, as might be the case in a Broadway show medley, for example. If the rhythm section can't play it, nobody else has a chance.

The rhythm section rehearsal

In a standard jazz/rock band set-up, you would expect:

- Drums (plus optional percussion)
- Bass (this might be bass guitar, string bass, or even tuba)
- Keyboard (piano or electric keyboard/synthesiser)
- Guitar (acoustic and/or electric).

Although we usually think of the drums as providing the rhythm, in most cases it is actually the bass player who provides the groove (see Part IV, Chapter 9 for more details). So:

- Start with the bass and drums, confirming that the lines are correct, not just the notes but also the phrasing and articulation.
- Work with the drummer to devise something which will be effective. You should also consider the choice of sticks. Would soft beaters work better here, or brushes? Discuss it with your player and make sure they feel involved in the decision.
- At this stage, any complex rhythms can be dealt with using the same approaches as outlined above. However, be wary of over-challenging your inexperienced players who may not be quite up to the task yet. There is little point in making them learn something which is beyond them, especially as it is likely to cause problems for the rest of the band later on. Far better to find an effective but simplified drum/bass pattern which still does the same job and creates the same feel (or at least does not do any damage).
- Add the percussion. Aim to ensure that the line(s) do not simply double the drum part but offer something different. In most cases you will be looking for additional colour and some attempt at location setting, such as claves for South America, tabla for India, bongos for a 1960s' spy theme. Use the rehearsal time to experiment with different instruments if they are available: small or large triangles perhaps, or higher pitched maracas. This is your chance as the director to get the feel as you want it, so make sure you use the opportunity.
- Add the guitar and/or keyboard. In many cases these two instruments will have similar music to play at the same time, so concentrate on getting your players to avoid duplication. Thus the piano and guitar may not play the written parts – often just chord sequences – but will aim to create a composite rhythmic pattern between them. It is often wise to divide the work between the two players, with one dropping out while the other plays before reversing the roles.

Spending time with the rhythm section – either separately or as part of the full rehearsal – can only ever be a good thing. Once these key players know what they are doing and what they are trying to achieve they will start to work as a team, and the effect on the rest of the group will be transforming. All of those niggles of tempo and rhythm will miraculously vanish and the rest of the group can sit on top of the newly-oiled engine and finally begin to sound like that samba band you were hoping for.

Medleys, and how to approach them

Selections from shows and films are staple amateur band repertoire, as they guarantee the ideal combination of a variety of styles and listener recognition. A West End or Broadway medley is the ideal concert starter or finisher, and there is plenty of music to explore.

However, such medleys are far from easy as your group will need to be much more chameleon-like, switching from a classic Viennese waltz to a samba to a big-band shout chorus in the space of a few bars. This puts a good deal of pressure on the rhythm section, who must be able to click instantly into the appropriate style, and on you, who must understand every song and know how to convey it (see Chapter 5).

Whatever you do, don't try to run one song into another at this stage – that will come later. Focus instead on getting the right tempo and feel for each separate song, so everyone knows what they are trying to achieve, and how to get the style right. It does not matter what comes before or after, or how logical the link is; the arranger has made that decision already, but each song still needs to live and have its own personality. Consider this: there is no musical connection between 'Waterloo', 'The Winner Takes It All' and 'Thank You for the Music' in an Abba medley – they are all different songs with different characters and must be treated as such. The transition from one to the next is just an arranging mechanism, no more, no less. At this stage in the rehearsal process, practise each song separately.

Cutting sections

Just because you have the printed score in front of you, it does not mean that you have to perform all of it. There are at least three reasons why you might consider cutting a section:

1. **Excessive and unnecessary length:** either because the piece overstays its welcome, or due to an imposed time limit (from an event organiser, for example). Your listeners will also influence your decision – there is little point in performing a 40-minute classical piece for an audience of primary school children, so just select part of it.
2. **Tricky sections:** your group should be able to give a decent performance of 80% of the work, but the 'presto vivace' section, for example, in the

middle will inevitably be beyond them, no matter how much practice you all do. Either you drop the piece altogether, which would be a shame as much of it will be successful and rewarding, or you take it on, secure in the knowledge that this section will be omitted from day one.

3. **Solo features:** this is similar to the above – if there is an exposed and lengthy trumpet or oboe solo halfway through, it is unlikely that your inexperienced player will rise to the challenge, especially with an audience present. However, this decision does not necessarily need to be made early in the rehearsal process – your soloist might surprise you – but in the back of your mind you should always have the option to make a cut.

Judicious cutting can also remove unwanted songs in a medley (there is always one nobody knows) or unnecessary repeats.

What if the cuts don't work, or sound wrong?
Unless you are very fortunate, it is unlikely that you will simply be able to jump from bar 24 to bar 82 without anybody noticing unless you are prepared to do a little adapting. There are three possible options, depending on the musical style:

1. **Devise a perfect cadence in the key you are going to:** in the run-up to the section where you wish to re-enter, use your knowledge of basic harmony to create a convincing perfect cadence – ideally with a dominant 7th chord before the entry (see Chapter 9 for more explanation) – by changing a few notes in each part. You will need to work this out in advance of the rehearsal but it is not too hard for each individual to alter their notes provided you are clear what you want. Do it well and the audience will never know.

2. **Unpitched percussion solo:** exploiting the fact that the drums/cymbals do not have definite pitch, in popular music it is possible to add a strategic solo into the proceedings of sufficient length for the listeners' ears to forget what key we have been in. The subsequent return of the band in the new key will not be quite so jarring as it might otherwise have been.

3. **Silence:** in some cases, notably when the music is very dramatic, you can use an extended silence to change key. In effect, you are making a point of the sudden modulation rather than hiding it, but once again without the harmonic jarring.

Used skilfully, all of the above have their place in a variety of performance situations and should always be considered if and when a potential problem is encountered.

Adding and doubling

Cutting may seem the obvious approach, but sadly it is not always an option.
No matter how tricky and exposed it is, you cannot ignore the fact that the
flute solo has a crucial melody to deliver – the main theme in a symphonic
movement perhaps, or 'Memory' in a selection from *Cats*. Somehow it just has
to happen or you will have to reject the whole piece.

In this situation consider simplifying, or even doubling a key line with another
strong player/instrument. You might add your violin leader to the flute line,
or a saxophone to help out a nervy French horn player. Provided you choose
instruments that blend well together there should be no problem. Discretion
may also be advisable in certain cases – you don't want to upset anyone. Who
knows, as rehearsals progress that soloist may surprise everyone (including
themselves) and by the time the concert arrives everything will be back to
normal.

*Isn't all this adaptation wrong? Shouldn't we aim to perform the music as the
composer intended?*
Of course you should. But remember, it is highly unlikely that the piece you are
attempting was originally intended for an inexperienced adult orchestra with
just three violins, one oboe, one French horn and no bassoon. Yes, you do have
the option of rejecting the piece altogether and existing purely on music written
for players of below Grade 5 standard – in which case you will quickly lose
the interest of your decent performers – or even arranging the music yourself.
However, with some smart adapting you will be able to perform rewarding
music, enabling your top players to shine while taking the pressure off the
weaker ones. You might upset a few purists, but at least you'll be trying to
perform decent music as well as possible and that is a laudable aim.

Remembering lip

Inexperienced brass and wind players get tired, so try to take that into account
when you are rehearsing instrumental groups. With tricky rhythmic passages,
instead of playing get them to clap or even sing the lines to learn them, and
remind your top trumpeters and trombonists to practise high parts down the
octave where it is more comfortable. And, of course, try to ensure that you
rehearse different sections at different times to give everyone a break. You will
need to make a conscious effort to do this at the start, but after a while it should
become second nature.

Perhaps the most important aspect is to talk to your players during rehearsals.
The questions 'How is your lip feeling? Are you OK to give that section another
go or do you want a rest?' will be greatly appreciated and will usually result in
much more effective music making.

FOR CHORAL GROUPS ONLY

Reading music

Although this is not essential it is always a good idea to encourage reading music by providing sheet music. It will not necessarily improve your singers' voices but it will certainly make them faster learners if there are music readers dotted around the sections. And faster learning means more songs being worked on, making it more likely that the good people will stay with you as they won't get bored and frustrated. Encourage all your singers to learn to read music, even if it is only a case of 'does it go up, down or stay the same?'. They will soon get the hang of it.

Exploring the use of the space with choral groups

This approach is especially good for choirs[†] which are used to sitting/standing in regimented lines or section blocks. Quite simply, put them in different places in the room. You might do it for musical reasons, perhaps to test them, or maybe just to keep everyone awake. Whatever the thought behind it, aim to move your singers around the space. Some suggestions:

- **Antiphony:** this is where the sections stand opposite each other to create a stereo effect. It can be particularly powerful in confrontational/argument songs, or even just question-and-answer as in the 'Tonight Quintet' from *West Side Story*, or the Gershwins' 'Let's Call the Whole Thing Off' ('you say eether, I say either').
- **Mixing:** asking people to stand next to others who are singing other parts. This situation is common in musical theatre, where the stage director is unlikely to stand all the sopranos together apart from through coincidence. Transferring this scenario to a choir rehearsal can often produce some interesting results.
- **Communal solos:** everyone is spread out around the space and not directly next to anyone at all – you are effectively faced with a set of soloists. With the addition of a backing track or rehearsal pianist you are now free to weave your way round the room to hear exactly what is happening with each individual.

Clearly you have to be careful with the way you use the above approaches. They are unlikely to work until most people are reasonably confident so, ideally, you should reserve these techniques for the end of the rehearsal sequence, when everybody feels they know the music really well and some may even be

---

† Many of the above ideas would work very well with instrumental groups if it wasn't for the fact that each player would need individual sheet music and they can rarely move when playing. It is much more common for players to share stands, so they rarely need a piece of music each. However, if that is not an issue, by all means try some of the ideas above with your classical orchestra and see what happens.

beginning to switch off in practices, convinced that they've got it all sorted. That is when mixing them all up really has an effect, and can often produce just the last-ditch push you were hoping for as some singers realise that perhaps they are not as note/word-perfect as they thought without their talented friend standing next to them, and a little more personal practice might not go amiss.

Movements and actions in rehearsal

Your choir may include some sort of choreography in performance. This book will not address dance moves, but the inclusion of choreography may affect your choice of repertoire (see Chapter 4). Some songs don't really work without dance moves, so if you don't want your choir to dance, don't choose them. Examples might be 'YMCA' or 'You Can't Stop the Beat' from *Hairspray*. Beware of songs that actually mention dancing in their lyrics – it will look very odd if everyone on stage stands stock still while singing 'I Love to Boogie' by T. Rex, or Abba's 'Dancing Queen'. Dance routines are great, but do be wary of how long they take to learn with amateurs and devise your rehearsal schedule accordingly.

In addition to choreographed steps and moves, there are many other ways to encourage movement from your singers during rehearsal. These actions will not make it to the performance so do not need to be drilled, but children and young people find them useful and amusing. They also work surprisingly well with adults. Examples might be:

- **Marching:** if you are singing a marching song, such as 'Come Follow the Band' from *Barnum*, ask everyone to march round the room while singing it. This process will certainly cement both the rhythm and meaning of the song very quickly.
- **Clapping:** frequently seen in performance, though not always done well, clapping is crucial for feeling the offbeats (2 and 4) in popular music and jazz. Finger clicking is even smarter and has the same result.[†]
- **Standing and sitting:** tell everyone to sit, and ask them to stand only when they are singing the tune and sit when they have the accompaniment. This always works well – you could even make it more sophisticated by requesting each section to stand when they have the fugue subject in a Bach oratorio, for example. Not only is this fun, it also strengthens everyone's structural knowledge of the piece, meaning they are much more likely to get those contrapuntal entries right without your help.
- **Air drumming:** this is great fun, with everyone seated at their imaginary rock drum kit and beating out the fills, but it can also serve a purpose.

---

† Useful tip: when recording a piece which requires any sort of clapping or finger clicking, aim to have as few as possible in your group actually doing those actions. This will improve the clarity of the finished result and prevent the frustration of trying (and failing) to get 30 people to clap at exactly the same time.

Many rock and jazz songs include awkward syncopated entries for the choir, either just before or just after the prevailing beat. Sadly these are often poorly delivered, so feeling the drum patterns (which may be real or invented) leading into these entries can enhance their crispness in performance. Your audience members will never know that every singer is secretly performing a mental drum fill in their heads in the rests, but they will be stunned by the clarity and punch of the subsequent offbeat choral entry. An example might be the lead-in to 'I'll make a brand new start of it' in the middle of Sinatra's 'New York, New York': the right mental drum fill (da, duh-duh-duh, *dum*!) should lead to a perfect entry.

As mentioned at the start of this chapter, the ongoing rehearsal sequence is arguably the most interesting part of the process. It should be by turns:

- **Constructive**: there should be a clear strategy for each practice, and the evidence of success should be there at the end.
- **Positive**: aim to balance any criticism with praise.
- **Varied**: as we have seen, there are many different ways of achieving your goals.
- **Experimental**: aim to instil a sense that anything might happen from week to week as you explore the music from all angles.
- **Off the wall**: unpredictability is good, and you should always be looking for a new approach (even if sometimes it doesn't work).
- **Informative**: throughout the process you will be aiming to teach your players good, lasting habits and helping them to learn a bit more about the musical styles you are trying to emulate.
- **Fun**: there should be plenty of laughs along the way.

And remember, always stay focused on successful music making as the ultimate goal. Your members will soon get fed up of being asked to undergo mad activities for no apparent reason, led by a director who appears to be doing things merely for the sake of them. You must always make it clear *why* you are asking them to do things, and what positive effect they will have on the eventual musical performance.

Above all, it is the constant creativity that matters, an ongoing desire to explore the music from a variety of viewpoints. This creativity, combined with a forensic attention to detail from you and your ever-alert ears, should lead to an imaginative, exhilarating and memorable performance.

The following chapter provides advice for the imminent concert and a suggested approach for the final rehearsal stage.

CHORAL STYLES ARRANGING
ANNING VENUE VOCALS DYNAMICS
CONDUCTING ADMINISTRATION
VENUE SOUND DYNAMICS MANAGING
JP TEACHING CONDUCTING L NG
FORMANCE PRACTICALITIES
TING T GV
ENUE DYNAMICS MANAGING CHORAL
RCUSSION INST
P LIGHTING SCORING STYLES

CASE STUDY:
PETER STARK, ERNEST READ
SYMPHONY ORCHESTRA

Who are you?
Peter Stark, Professor of Conducting,
Royal College of Music; Rehearsal
Conductor, European Union Youth
Orchestra; Conductor-in-Residence,
National Youth Orchestra; Mentor for the
BBC's *Maestro!* reality series.

Also a freelance conductor and teacher,
having worked with professional,
student and youth orchestras.

What was the ensemble?
The Ernest Read Symphony Orchestra (1989–2009).

IN THE BEGINNING

Who did you expect your audience to be?
With concerts in Waterloo we hoped to attract tourists, but the bulk of the
audience was always friends and families of the players.

What was your unique selling point?
The history of the organisation, and the legacy of Ernest Read.

What were your criteria for success? Did you have a one-year/five-year plan?
Probably a two-year plan – the success criteria were based on the satisfaction
of the players.

Advertising: how did you do it?
Web advertising and word of mouth.

THE ONGOING PROCESS

Did you audition?
No.

Venue: how and why did you choose it?
Central London – convenient for players and audience.

Funding: what system did you have?
Subscriptions and ticket income.

Did you have any assistants at rehearsals?
For the last four years of my time we chose an assistant conductor (by audition) to take rehearsals and conduct occasional pieces in concert.

What about administration?
This was done by a voluntary committee.

To what extent did your original plan change from the start?
There was a continual evolution, so difficult to quantify, but no dramatic changes.

What difficulties have you encountered?
Audience numbers and funding.

What advice would you give to someone else considering a similar venture?
Go for it! If your heart is in it you will succeed.

What key tips can you pass on about organising ensemble rehearsals?
- Never compromise the greatness of the music; great music is *not* just the province of great musicians.
- Never assume that your players are not good enough to do it better.

And in performance?
The conductor should enable the players to play better than their own perceived capability, and respect their contribution at all times. This doesn't mean not being hard, or demanding, but conscious of their levels of achievement.

Who are your musical heroes?
Carlos Kleiber, Bruno Walter, Klaus Tennstedt, Reginald Goodall, Count Basie. Every musical child and the parents that support them.

With a week to go your rehearsal strategy needs to change. From this point the priority is simple: to get from A to Z and finish. All the detailed work should have been done, it should now just be a case of topping and tailing and ensuring that everyone is clear what is happening and when, in terms of both the music and administration. However, even at this late stage, it is remarkable how much last-minute improvement can be made.

THE LAST REHEARSAL PRIOR TO THE PERFORMANCE

This should really be considered the final rehearsal, as it is unlikely you will have time for much genuine practising on the day in your venue, assuming you are fortunate enough to get access before you perform. At most competitions and festivals you will not be able to get on the stage until the moment of truth.

What should I do in this session? Are run-throughs the best approach?
In an ideal world you will have time to run everything, but your real priority is to clarify things and remove any possible confusions which will manifest themselves all too clearly under the pressure of performance. Some suggestions:

- **Beginnings:** make sure everyone is clear what you are counting and that they know how many beats they will get before they come in at the start of each piece/section. This is much more important than you might think, particularly if you have extras joining you at the last minute – and it can cause chaos if not checked. Once it is confirmed exactly what is happening, especially when there are several changes of speed and time signature in the piece, you should mark it in the score and stick to it.
- **Endings:** assuming you are expecting applause at the end, it is essential that everyone finishes confidently and together: you can never over-rehearse the final bars. Start from the end of each piece and work backwards. A clean ending never fails to generate an audience response.
- **Transitions:** as discussed above, in the early stages of rehearsing a medley or linked suite of pieces, you should treat each section as a separate entity and not worry about how one leads into another. By this

point that will have changed and you will have had several run-throughs of the whole piece, but it is still wise to check each join. Practise running from one tempo/feel into another, no more than a few bars at a time. Any such joins are potentially the most difficult moments for a conductor in performance, so it is worth spending some time on this particular aspect of your role.

Attention to detail: it's never too late

Keep listening to what is *actually* happening in front of you, and not just what you *think* is happening.

- Are the dynamics really contrasted enough? *You* may know they are there, but will the audience pick them up?
- What is the balance really like? You may have worked at it for weeks now, but has it made any difference?
- Is the rhythm section solid, or are there moments where the tempo still seems to fluctuate?
- Is that tricky soprano entry now sorted out, or is there still some uncertainty?
- Are the words clear enough, and does everybody know them?

If you are not happy with something, do your best to deal with it. You might also factor in the upcoming venue itself and what effect it will have on the sound you are hearing now. Hopefully life will be easier at the performance. Your school/church hall is unlikely to match a theatre acoustic, for example, but might the sense of the words be lost in a more resonant building?

ADMINISTRATION

This may seem unnecessary when you have so much else to think about, but it is vital. By all means delegate this to someone else if you can but, as the director of the rehearsal, you need to build in time to allow for this part of the process. Ensure you reinforce and provide answers to the following:

- What time does the concert start, and where is it?
- Will there be a sufficient gap between the rehearsal and the concert, allowing people time to go home?
- If people are staying, as is often the case with adults who live some distance from the venue or youngsters who cannot get picked up, is there somewhere to rest and change, or will they need to make their own arrangements?

- What should they be wearing? This should have been discussed at an earlier practice, but it is always worth confirming.
- What will they need to bring on the day/night? Will you have their music, or will they have taken it home to practise? For instrumentalists, will they need to bring their own music stands or will they be provided at the venue? Somebody may also need to organise clothes pegs for the music if the event is outdoors.
- Tickets: will any be available on the door and at what prices?
- What time will the event finish? Will the performers be free to go immediately or are you expecting people to help clear up afterwards?
- Will photos or videos be allowed? If there are children involved, you will need written permission from their parents.

If the performance involves children or young people you should have sent out a letter in advance, but it is still worth checking that it reached home and whether there are any matters arising; some parents will still have surprisingly little idea what is happening, and you will usually get the blame.

There is nothing worse than being fully prepared musically for a public performance, only to discover that someone has left their music at home and another has misunderstood the dress requirements and has arrived in trainers. It may seem amusing on paper, but in practice it results in a huge amount of unnecessary stress, so do everything you can to avoid it.

Always allow time for these administrative issues in the penultimate rehearsal – you will not regret it.

THE DAY OF THE PERFORMANCE: FINAL PRACTICE IN THE VENUE

As mentioned above there are several situations where it is impossible to rehearse at the venue before you perform: you might be on a bandstand, in a marquee, in the middle of a shopping centre or even in a field. In these situations you just have to do your best, having factored the knowledge of the performance location into all of your rehearsals and prepared your performers accordingly.

However, even with proper venues it is not as simple as you might think. Unless you are very fortunate it is unlikely that you will be able to rehearse on the actual stage until the day of the performance itself. Even if the event is in another part of a school where you practise, such as the theatre, you will probably not have been in there as it will either have been in use for other activities or simply locked. It is therefore vital that you make the most of the opportunity to be in there and see how it sounds.

Extras

Although you may not be planning this at the start of the process, in practice it is likely that you will choose to bring in extra players/singers to boost your group's performance. There are various legitimate reasons for this:

- A key person may drop out, either through illness or another commitment
- Despite your best efforts, your initial recruitment may have failed to attract sufficient players in a crucial section of your band/orchestra
- There may be balance issues, especially with male/female choir ratios.

There is nothing wrong with bringing in extras late in the process, provided you are doing it for the overall musical good of the group. You should also let the group know in advance that you are planning to do this so as not to upset anyone. In general, people will be delighted and relieved – the lone tenor in your choir will be looking forward to the concert much more when he knows there will be someone else alongside him.

Any extras you bring in must be capable, experienced and reliable. If a friend kindly offers to help you out, decide whether to accept or not purely on musical grounds. There is nothing worse than finding oneself next to an extra who is no better than you are and is adding little to the overall performance. Any extra has a clear responsibility to lead and enhance, so choose carefully.

Unless they are genuine professionals or know the work back to front, you should expect all extras to attend the rehearsal on the day at the very least. Those who promise to turn up for the concert only should be treated with caution; even if they do know the piece, they cannot possibly know how you are going to conduct it. There is also the uncertainty – will this individual actually show up on the night?

In the end it is entirely your call and you should do whatever you feel you must to get the best performance out of the group as a whole. However, in the long run your aim must be for your group to become self-sufficient.

Stage management

How many chairs and stands do you need, and where are they coming from? It is not as straightforward as it sounds, especially when people miss the final rehearsal and then turn up on the evening, expecting somewhere to sit. If possible, get someone to sketch a plan of the layout, including absentees.

When you have established what is needed, you also need to check how it will happen, and whose responsibility it is.

Lighting

This is not about spectacular mirror ball effects or whirling spotlights, it is much more basic than that:

Can the performers see the music, and will the audience be able to see them? Remember, particularly in the winter months, it will be very dark early in the evening, and any extraneous light from the daytime rehearsal will have completely disappeared. If you have not planned ahead, your performers will get a shock when they discover they cannot see the music and the venue's lighting technician has left everything set up and gone home. Also, beware the single sheet of music on the wire mesh stand which becomes transparent when the light reflects through it. A simple solution is to place some card or a folder on the stand behind the music.

Note to all choir directors: *don't forget the pianist*. You may well want to start or end with a dramatic blackout/fade to black, a technique which will work fine in the afternoon rehearsal. By the evening, however, with no light filtering through the windows and no side door accidentally left open, it could well be too dark even to see the keyboard (let alone the music) and, unless the pianist has memorised those few bars, disaster will ensue. Always make sure the piano is partially lit by the lighting team, or provide the pianist with their own light.

Sound and listening

Forget microphones for the moment – what does your ensemble actually sound like in the venue, and what is the balance like? There is only one way to find this out – start the group off, and then leave them to it while you wander round the hall/theatre to hear it from the audience's point of view. Is it just a mush of sound? Can you hear the words? Is the bass player too loud? These questions can only be answered by you as you move around the venue, and it is a very important thing to do, if only out of respect for your audience.

If you are using microphones and/or some sort of sound system, it is vital that a proper sound check has occurred – you cannot just trust to luck – and you need to build in time for this. Vocals are the most crucial – they must not be drowned by over-excited guitarists or drummers, and it would be nice if the audience can understand the words as well. Remember, no audience member in history has ever complained that they could hear the words *too* clearly.

Presentation

If presentation – usually choreography – is a key part of your overall performance you will have been practising it for several weeks. However, if not, this is emphatically not the moment to try anything new. Just make sure of the following:

- **Stage entry**: everyone knows where they are lining up to come onto the stage, and in what order.
- **Movement during the performance**: singers may need to reconfigure their layout for a particular song, or the percussion section may well need to switch instruments between numbers.
- **Stage exit**: any bows, either as a unit or for individuals, and which side of the stage performers should exit.

This all helps to make things look more professional, although it is not a substitute for getting the music right.

Run-throughs

Assuming you have time after all of the above, aim to run through everything, without stopping, at least once: it just makes everyone feel better. However, if the clock is against you, don't panic. Concentrate on starts, endings and tricky links – they should know the rest by now really.

THE PERFORMANCE ITSELF: THE ROLE OF THE CONDUCTOR

'Preparation is everything ... if you have rehearsed properly, you should be able to enjoy the concert because the work is done.'
(Sir Georg Solti, quoted in *Orchestra!* by J. Younghusband, 1991)

Arguably, provided you have had a series of successful rehearsals and everyone knows what they have to do you might be excused for thinking: shouldn't they be able to do it without me? The answer:

Yes, they should be able to do it without you, but not as well as they can with you there.

You are their leader, the person who motivates and inspires them and gives them the confidence they need to give of their best. You are also the person they look up to, and have done over the last ten weeks. You have encouraged them to get through tricky situations when the notes wouldn't come and everything seemed lost. Above all, you have persevered with them, acknowledging their shortcomings and pushing them to overcome them. In short, they believe they need you.

In practical terms you are there to:

- Keep everyone together
- Make the transitions between styles/tempi as clean as possible
- Give confidence, especially by cueing entries and providing a clear beat
- Deal with live errors, and make sure the music keeps going
- Inspire your performers to do their best, and sometimes to play above themselves.

Talking to the audience

When performing to people who may not be regular concert-goers it is a good idea to put your audience members at their ease as much as possible. If your group consists of adults there may well be young children and teenagers in your audience, dragged along reluctantly to watch mum or dad. They will not be used to this and may feel embarrassed in such an alien environment.

How much you talk depends on your confidence as a public speaker. You might just discuss the pieces you are doing, perhaps drawing attention to particular featured individuals or sections, or you might be a little bit more chatty – anecdotes derived from the rehearsal process always go down well. You will know who can take a bit of gentle teasing by now.

There is also a strategic reason for talking to the audience: it gives your performers a break. This is particularly important for inexperienced brass players (see 'Remembering lip' in Chapter 6) – they will be grateful for the hiatus and will play better as a result. It should not be between every piece, however. A good plan is to talk about the next two pieces, or even to refer back to the piece you have just played. Very well-known music – the James Bond theme, for example – does not need any explanation in advance.

As the conductor you do matter in performance and you can make a difference. But, on a basic level, you and the performers have a job to do. Assuming you have rehearsed effectively, creatively and efficiently, and your performers believe in you, everything should be fine.

If a few minor things go wrong, don't worry. The audience members will either not notice – after all, they don't know what was meant to happen – or they are just as likely not to care. It is the overall impact of the performance that matters.

POST-PERFORMANCE ANALYSIS

Once the performance is over and the dust has settled, you should attempt to work out how it went, and why. It is vital that you assess the good and bad. It is all too easy to focus on the negatives, but there will be a lot of good things:

- What worked really well?
- What did you do that you will definitely do again?

Identifying aspects and types of pieces that worked well – either with the group or the audience – is a key part of your role as a group leader. You are clearly going to look to do more of the same in the future, and it is a strong basis on which to start your programme planning.

However, inevitably there will have been some moments when things did not go exactly as planned, and these will usually be down to a few key factors:

- **Performers' inexperience:** your group is just not used to performing in public and dealing with the associated nerves. The members will learn and improve over time.
- **Difficulty of repertoire:** was it just too hard at this stage in the group's development? Or, despite the occasional mistakes, is it still worthwhile pursuing this policy, accepting that it might take time but will be worth it in the end? Discuss it informally with the rest of the group, especially your more experienced people. What do they think?

You yourself may be another factor:

- Did you know the music well enough? Could you have been better prepared?
- Did you get all your count-ins right? What about the tempos?
- Would you do anything differently next time, either in the performance itself or during the earlier rehearsal process?

Having said all of the above, try not to be too down on yourself, especially if you have not been conducting for long. Just like your members, you will get better as long as you learn from your mistakes.

Self-criticism is neither easy nor pleasant – you will always get well-meaning friends and family telling you not to worry – but it is the *only way to get better*. Any improvements can only really come from you, and an improving group will attract better and more experienced performers as word gets round that your so-called beginner band or choir is actually coming along surprisingly well and your weekly rehearsal slot is becoming the place to be.

PART IV:
ARRANGING FOR YOUR ENSEMBLE

'It was like a gigantic crossword puzzle or a jigsaw with all the pieces that had to be put together.'

(Sebesky, 1994)

Thus Don Sebesky describes his first attempts at the mysterious and much-misunderstood art of musical arranging. In his case it was for the jazz orchestra, but it could just as easily be applied to classical orchestras, wind bands, brass bands and choirs, indeed, any musical ensemble consisting of several instruments or voices, used separately or in combination.

To the general public, the arranger/orchestrator is anonymous. People talk of Schoenberg's *Les Misérables*, not John Cameron's powerful orchestral sound; The Beatles' 'Eleanor Rigby', not (Sir) George Martin's strings; Frank Sinatra's 'Come Fly With Me', with no mention of Billy May; and the hills may still be alive with Richard Rodgers' *Sound of Music*, but not Robert Russell Bennett's. In recent times the conductor John Wilson has highlighted and revisited the work of the Hollywood and Broadway dance arrangers; composers such as Gershwin, Berlin, Kern and Porter may well have written the original melodies, but it was men and women such as Conrad Salinger, Leo Arnaud, Skip Martin, André Previn, Trudy Rittmann and numerous uncredited staff arrangers who took these 32-bar tunes and extended them into sophisticated, lengthy and exhilarating production numbers for the stage and screen, work that is carried on today by names such as David Chase and Mark Hummel.

The final section of this book deals in detail with the technique of arranging music for amateur ensembles, culminating in two specific arranging tasks: a choral folk song setting and a theme and variations.

Although every aspect has been addressed systematically, a reasonable standard of musical literacy is assumed from the reader at this point. Although it is quite possible to arrange by ear for a small group, as numerous jazz **head arrangements** have proved, such a free approach is not practical for larger ensembles.

Thus the following chapters discuss chord sequences, key changes and cadences, and this is unavoidable. As the eminent musical theatre composer Stephen Sondheim explains in the 'reintroduction' to his latest book, *Look, I Made A Hat*, in response to criticism that his previous book, *Finishing The Hat*, had addressed the detailed aspects of lyric writing but not composing:

'... the technique of composition is impossible to be precise and articulate about without using jargon ... understanding what a perfect rhyme is requires no special knowledge. But understanding what a perfect cadence is requires knowing something about harmony and the diatonic scale.'

(Sondheim, 2011)

To Sondheim, 'music is a foreign language which everyone knows but only musicians can speak. The effect is describable in everyday language; how to achieve it is not'.

Thus, like Sondheim, we make no apologies for the technical language which follows: there is no other way to explain the arranger's art.

'YOU KNOW ENOUGH ALREADY to do good arrangements.'

(Runswick, 1992; his capitals)

'Good arrangers are, for the most part, made, not born.'

(Sebesky, 1994)

There is a huge amount of commercial music available for choirs and instrumental ensembles of varying levels of difficulty. Much of it is excellent, but it all has one flaw: *None of it was written specifically for your group.*

As the group leader, your main job is to make your ensemble sound as good as possible, and learning to arrange specifically for the strengths of your singers and players should only ever lead to a positive outcome. No longer will you need to fret over choosing pieces or whether your trumpeters or cellists will be able to play their parts: you will have made certain that they can already, and the result will be musically satisfying for all.

In addition to the above, other reasons to arrange for your ensemble might be:

- An opportunity to perform music not otherwise available. If your choir wishes to perform a lesser-known folk song, and there is no suitable version on the market, you can solve that problem.
- A chance to do it the way you think it should be done. How many times have you sat in performance thinking: 'Why did the arranger think this version of the tune would work?'
- It makes your group unique and interesting. No other group in the area can perform this piece, so if the public wants to hear it they have to listen to you. The more you arrange, the more people will appreciate that your performances are unique events.
- It can save money, at least at the start. Unless you are going to insist on a fee for your time, arranging is a great way to create or reinforce your group's repertoire at little or no cost.
- You are driven to do it. As you become more experienced in the arranger's art you will not be able to stop yourself.

THE DIFFERENCE BETWEEN COMPOSING AND ARRANGING

In the simplest terms, composing involves an original melodic/thematic idea of *your invention*, whereas arranging is working with *other people's* pre-written music. After that stage the techniques required are very similar. In this chapter you will find plenty of strategies and tips but, in the end, it all comes down to experience and a willingness to learn from your mistakes. You must write a draft, rehearse it with your singers/players, rewrite, put it in front of an audience, see what works and what doesn't, learn from it, and keep writing.

THE DIFFERENCE BETWEEN INSTRUMENTATION AND SCORING

- **Instrumentation:** these are the instruments/voices you have at your disposal. It may be a standard line-up such as a chamber orchestra, or a more unorthodox grouping arising from necessity, such as a wind band with no bassoons and only one French horn.
- **Scoring:** deciding what to do with your available instruments/voices, when and why. Who will get the tune, who will provide the accompaniment, and when will the roles change? And just because they are there does not mean all the available instruments need to be used all the time.

WHAT YOU NEED TO KNOW

To the beginner it may seem as if you have to know everything about every instrument before you can arrange effectively for an ensemble. This is probably true at professional level, but at amateur level you should do your best with what you know already and aim to keep learning.

Let's say you are a flautist. Much of your knowledge will be transferable to the other wind instruments, including saxophones. The brass section may be less familiar, but at least you understand about breathing and phrasing.

- **Singers:** you are already knowledgeable about the basics of all voices: range, projection, breathing and support. You also know quite a bit about harmony.
- **Pianists:** you may be limited in your knowledge of other instruments, but you are probably strong on harmony, an essential part of the arranger's art.
- **Percussionists:** you may not feel in such a strong position, until you realise that hardly anyone else knows about percussion and what it can do.

Although there is no need to be an expert in everything at the start of the process, as you produce more arrangements you will need to develop a working knowledge of everything you are writing for. Much of this will happen in rehearsals – your singers or players will quickly tell you if something does not work and will hopefully propose a more practical solution. However, there are certain elements which will help:

- Learn to write *idiomatically*, (for the specific instrument concerned). At the start this may be a series of purely negative responses (I won't do that again) but there is also room for learning what works well on certain instruments, for example, rapid tremolo string writing cannot be successfully replicated by any other instrument.
- Develop your knowledge of the rhythm section and percussion. Unless you run an a cappella choir the percussion will frequently be a vital element of any arrangement you do, providing both rhythm and colour.
- Listen! As always, the ears are the most important tools for an arranger, so you should be on the alert at all times. Instead of just counting bars rest in rehearsals – very common if you are a brass player, for example – listen to the other sections of the group and the effects that are being created. If possible, borrow the scores from the conductor you are working with; you might even chat to them about specifics of instrumentation. Try to mix up your listening, aiming for a combination of live (from a position in the middle of the group) and recordings.

WHERE TO START

Imagine you are working for a client, in this case yourself. What are your requirements? This is a really useful exercise, as it forces you to focus on what is needed. You should always arrange with a specific performance in mind.

Some possible questions:

- **How long should it be?** Is this going to be a short item, or something more substantial?
- **Where will it be done?** The performance venue has a major impact on the sound of your group, so you need to bear it in mind when arranging. Is it large or small? Resonant or dry?
- **Will you have access to other equipment** such as lighting or microphones? If so, you might consider making use of these if you can, and it will affect what and how you write.
- **Will it ever be repeatable in any other context?** This is an important consideration. If the piece is to go into your group's standard repertoire it will need to be versatile. In general, aim for this approach, although there will always be exceptions, such as the opportunity to arrange something for a prestigious occasion. In which case, might you need

to do a simplified version and ensure that works as well? As has been demonstrated by MTV's 'Unplugged' concept and the Radio 1 *Live Lounge* series, the same music can exist in several guises provided it is skilfully arranged.

- **Who is your audience?** Will this be performed in front of a sophisticated musical crowd or a group of friends? There is little point in arranging a 21st-century atonal masterpiece for the delight of your family, but equally a more educated audience might not be thrilled by your reggae approach to 'Baa Baa Black Sheep'.

WHERE WILL THE PIECE GO IN THE PROGRAMME?

Is the piece one of the following?

- **Opener** – which will probably mean it needs to be lively and catchy
- **Closer** – the final major item needs to be substantial and impressive
- **Light relief** – positioned either in the midst of the concert or as a bouncy encore
- **Calming interlude** – to break up a sequence of loud, lively pieces
- **Solo feature** – might this make it a one-off if the featured soloist leaves?
- **Demonstration/competition piece** – in this case, which particular strengths of your group do you need to show off?

COPYRIGHT: HOW IT WORKS

From the moment it is completed, the composer owns the rights to that piece of music. The same applies to the lyrics in the case of a song. Any performance royalties will go to the composer or, if deceased, the composer's estate.

In that case, is there anything to arrange?
There are at least two types of music readily accessible to you:

- **Traditional:** melodies and songs which have no acknowledged author. These might be folk songs, negro spirituals, nursery rhymes or Christmas carols.
- **In the public domain:** this expression refers to works written by composers who have been dead for 70 years, after which their work becomes public property. The most relevant example of this in popular music is George Gershwin (d. 1937).

So does that mean I can arrange any song by George Gershwin then?
Not quite. The *melodies* of Gershwin's songs are indeed out of copyright, but

the *lyrics* are not. This is because his long-time collaborator brother Ira (d. 1983) outlived George by 46 years. In other words, we can legitimately produce a version of the melody of 'Our Love is Here to Stay' without any qualms, but we would need to ask permission if we wanted it sung.

Copyright law is a minefield but not insurmountable; if you are in any doubt it is wise to check first. What are assumed to be traditional songs can be unexpectedly complicated. The folk song arrangement in Chapter 10 had to be carefully selected so as not to breach any copyrights, and even then there were several versions to choose from, only some of which were in the public domain.

Of course, if you do want to arrange something which is in copyright it is simple enough to approach the publishers and seek their permission. Unless you are planning to desecrate the original it is unlikely you would be turned down, although you may have to pay a fee for the privilege. It is also highly likely that the resulting arrangement will be licensed for use by your group only.

Further information on copyright is available on this book's companion website.

As a basic rule, there are two types of arranging:

1. **The cover version**: this is where you are aiming to replicate the original as closely as possible, albeit for a different instrumental combination. An example might be a simple 'Londonderry Air' for brass. There is no need to do anything clever here and people like hearing the familiar.
2. **The new/unexpected take**: here you attempt to put your own stamp on the tune, effectively turning it into something new and unique. Using 'Londonderry Air' as an example, might it work as a gentle bossa nova, or perhaps a march?

If your instant response to the above is 'No it wouldn't' you are probably right, and that is what makes this approach to arranging such a balancing act: you risk alienating your audience (and performers) by producing something that nobody likes because it does not feel right.

Yet this type of arranging can be the most rewarding and is certainly the most creative. It may not work all the time, and there are occasions when it is plainly a bad idea (few brides will appreciate a surprise jazz version of Mendelssohn's 'Wedding March' as they are walking up the aisle on their big day) but it is the essence of true arranging – the overwhelming desire to create something new.

'No matter how sensitive an arranger is, there will be times when he misjudges a voicing or effect; this is to be expected. If such were not the case, it would mean he had stopped experimenting ... This attitude must be avoided – it means the end of growth.'

(Sebesky, 1994)

This chapter has provided an outline of general approaches to arranging. In the next chapter we will cover the specific techniques of the arranger's art.

Unless you are very fortunate your group will usually consist of a mix of stronger members and weaker ones. This is where the skill of arranging really comes into its own, and once you understand its power you will never look back. With some smart arranging, this mix of abilities should never show. There are two simultaneous considerations:

1. **Featuring:** you know who your best people are, so make sure the audience hears plenty of them. Give them the tune, or solo sections, put the spotlight on them.

And at the same time:

2. **Protecting:** deliberately avoid drawing attention to your weaker players or singers. Eliminate exposed entries, or key moments, take the pressure off them, keep them in sensible ranges and ideal keys, use them effectively but discreetly.

This is the arranger's sleight of hand, the razzle-dazzle that sets your group apart from the rest. If done well, you are guaranteed successful performances every time.

It can be especially useful at youth level, where players outgrow your group and move on. Suddenly the piece that worked really well last year is no longer viable, as the solo trumpeter has left and there is no obvious replacement. However, one judicious piece of arranging later and the piece works equally well for saxophone or trombone. Or, if that proves impossible, you can arrange a different piece to feature this year's best player(s). Your group still sounds effective to the outsider and everyone applauds you for its consistency.

This last aspect is vital. Consistency is the hardest thing for any ensemble director to achieve, no matter how much one plans ahead. Arranging can, and will, get you off the hook and give you the breathing space until the next outstanding soloist comes along.

STRUCTURE

In order to be successful and appealing, your arrangements will need to be clearly structured. Of course, there are exceptions, but not for a beginner: you don't want to alienate everyone at the start of your arranging career. Stick to what people want, and play safe. There will be plenty of time to experiment later when you have established your credentials.

Let us consider the field of popular music. There are two main approaches:

- Verse/chorus: this is very satisfying, instantly providing the desired amount of repetition and contrast.
- Theme and variations: this is much more common for instrumental groups rather than choral, and is also very pleasing. The known tune is always present, but disguised (see Chapter 11 for instrumental variation techniques).

In addition to the above, you will need to master three other aspects of musical arranging:

- **Introductions:** not just at the start of the piece, but also in the middle, particularly when changing styles in a set of variations or medley.
- **Endings:** notably at the end of the whole piece, where the type of ending you choose will have a direct impact on the subsequent audience response.
- **Transitions/links:** unless you are going to stop and start all the time you will need to learn how to link sections together, ideally by using thematic material that has either been heard already or is about to appear.

Introductions

There are various types of introduction, all of which work in different ways. A comprehensive range of examples of types of introductions and endings can be found on the website accompanying this book, but the main approaches are:

1. **Generic:** in this introduction there is no clue as to what will come next – it will be a surprise. There is nothing inherently wrong with this approach, and it is very easy to do, but it does not really introduce the tune at all.
2. **Thematic:** here the introduction uses part of the upcoming tune so it becomes familiar. This approach is commonly used by church organists – in the play over – to remind the members of the congregation how the tune goes before they sing it. The thematic intro can be varied by using

other segments of the tune such as the end or even the middle, and thus an apparently generic approach is revealed as being the opposite by the time the melody has been heard once through.

3. **Atmospheric/evocative**: while there may not be a reference to the actual melody, the mood is set by the introduction, meaning that the arrival of the ensuing tune makes perfect sense to the ear.

4. **Chord sequence**: here there is no melody, but the underlying chord structure has already been introduced so when the tune arrives it sits on the top of the harmony.

5. **Straight in**: here the melody appears immediately, and it can be a very effective technique, if only because everyone is expecting some sort of introduction. However, in reality, it does not work well for choral groups as there is no obvious way of getting the starting note (unless you use a pitch pipe off stage). Such an approach can work well with experienced singers, but not with nervous amateurs.

6. **Shock/surprise**: here there is not so much a lack of clues as outright deception and irrelevance as to what follows. As a result of this disconnection, this technique is comparatively rare and worth explaining. Perhaps the ultimate example is the extraordinary (in all senses of the word) introduction to Michael Bublé's seminal recording of 'Cry Me a River'. As Bublé himself explains: 'I wrote that opening – what would you call it? a fanfare? overture? – and I wanted it to be John Williams-esque, very cinematic. That's where we started, and then David Foster wrote the rest of the arrangement.' The first few bars make no sense at all, and yet it somehow works. Indeed, in many ways, the introduction grew to have a life of its own, separate from the song, and the BBC used it as the title sequence of its Winter Olympics coverage in 2010.

The above approach, though tempting, is to be treated with great care. It can so easily go wrong and end up as a disconnected irrelevance. Definitely not for the beginner anyway.

To hear a less aggressive but equally effective demonstration of the power of the 'wrong' intro, listen to the recording of the 'New York, New York' medley by singer Mel Torme and pianist George Shearing. Shearing constantly plays the instantly recognisable introduction to Sinatra's 'New York, New York' but the twist is that Torme proceeds to sing various *other* songs after these lead-ins. The effect is both interesting and entertaining, and the live audience finds it very funny.

Any arranger must have the capacity to provide appropriate introductions to their work, and should also understand the response they will generate from the listener.

Endings

A weak ending can cause all sorts of problems. Hitherto well-written pieces can elicit muted responses from an audience, leaving the long-suffering arranger bemused and disappointed, when all that has happened is that the ending to the piece has been poorly constructed. A well-thought-out ending lets the audience know what to think and how (and when) to respond. There are five basic types:

1. **The push-button:** so called because it pushes the applause button. This technique, done well, will have the audience on its metaphorical feet even before the last chord has finished. Although this is a musical theatre term, classical composers are experts at it. This is clearly guaranteed to stop the show, so it must be used sparingly, especially in variation form where continuity is the key (although it can be used effectively to break the overall piece into two or three segments).

2. **The false ending:** effectively a planned encore, the audience is led to believe that the piece has finished – matched by the anticipated applause – before discovering that there is more to come. It is the musical equivalent of a stand-up comedian bidding goodnight before returning to do one or two more (pre-planned) jokes due to 'overwhelming' audience demand. Everyone is in on the twist, but it doesn't stop them playing along. Used sparingly, and with humour, the false ending can be an effective tool for the arranger.

3. **The fade:** beloved of pop producers, but it rarely works well in a live context. The audience is aware that we are reaching the end, but does not know when to clap, if at all. A live fade often results in a light smattering of applause and is unsatisfactory for all concerned. In a sense, everyone feels cheated: the performers feel distinctly underwhelmed by the apparent lack of enthusiasm, and the audience feels guilty and frustrated that it cannot show its proper appreciation. The only real opportunity to use the fade technique effectively is in the middle of a medley or set of variations, where one melody can drift into another, often with an element of surprise involved.

4. **The quiet conclusion:** there is no doubt that the piece has ended – in contrast to the fade – but the atmosphere is calm and relaxed, generating warm but controlled applause. There will be no unseemly cheering or standing ovation, as that is not what is needed at this point in the proceedings. Once again, the classical composers are the masters of this, especially at the conclusion of symphonic slow movements.

5. **The sudden halt:** in recent years this has become a common, almost clichéd, technique used by modern pop performers. Without any preamble the song just stops on an unexpected chord, the performer mumbles 'thank you' into the microphone, and the audience is expected to respond accordingly. This may work for a solo singer but it is unlikely to be as effective for an ensemble and, in most cases, should be avoided.

It is clear from the above that there is a variety of introductions and endings available to the arranger, and the decision as to which one is appropriate is usually related to the position of the piece in the overall concert programme. Thus a work positioned at the end of the first or second half would usually be expected to be rousing, generating plenty of instantaneous button-pushing applause, whereas a song placed in the middle of the second half and intended as a relaxing contrast might require a different approach.

Transitions/links

It is probably easiest to think of these as another way of using the various introductions and endings discussed in detail above. Thus the quiet conclusion of one section might lead gently into the next section, or you could exploit the element of surprise by switching to a totally different tempo or style, using the ensuing introduction to change gear. For more examples of the above, see Chapter 11.

OTHER ASPECTS TO CONSIDER

Length

When arranging anything, you must consider the length of your piece in comparison to the original. A folk song with three verses will probably end up being just that, with the possible addition of an introduction, a couple of links (perhaps to modulate) and an extended ending.

However, any work where a short idea is used as the basis for a more extended piece, such as a theme and variations or fantasia, will clearly be much longer than the original. At least one of the variations is likely to be slowed down, and there may also be occasions when the harmonic sequence is lengthened, meaning that it takes twice as many bars to complete the original melody. Any faster sections will be balanced by slower ones, and there is also likely to be an extended final variation to produce a satisfactory conclusion.

As always, there will be programme considerations to take into account. Is this piece intended to be a major item in the concert or merely a short filler? You will need to tailor your arrangement accordingly.

Percussion: why it is so important, and how to use it

For many amateur musicians the percussion section still holds a sense of mystery and mystique. On the one hand it looks so simple to do, and yet comparatively few are happy to write music for it or include it in performance. This is a great shame as it can be so effective when used well – few choral performances of 1960s' pop songs would not be enhanced by the discreet addition of a tambourine, and the same goes for medieval dances and tabor drums, flamenco plus castanets, and samba with additional maracas.

The use of percussion in any arrangement can add so much to the overall texture and colour, and it is an aspect that no true arranger can afford to do without. In essence there are two types:

1. **Rhythmic:** the percussion provides the basic rhythm of the piece – rock, swing, Latin American – to create the feel or groove. Much of this role is taken by the drum kit (see opposite).
2. **Colour/location:** in this case the percussion is used more to evoke a certain country/period/style. Examples include Spanish castanets, Caribbean steel drums and Indian tabla drums. It can be used as an effective shortcut for the ear – think repetitive tom-toms for a native American war dance, or bongos for a quasi *Mission Impossible* spy thriller.

Naturally the two styles above constantly interlock and overlap – in a samba, for example – providing an exhilarating combination of rhythm and colour. In many ways it is often best to regard the role of the percussion thus: how can I possibly create the effect I am looking for without it?

A second way of categorising percussion is whether it has definite pitch or not:

- **Untuned:** instruments that do not have identifiable pitches, although they can still be thought of as high and low. Examples include bass drums, snare/side drums, tambourines, triangles, cymbals, claves, woodblocks and tom-toms.
- **Tuned:** these instruments can produce specific pitches to order, and can therefore be used for melodic writing. The most common are timpani, xylophone and glockenspiel.

The drum kit

The standard drum kit is the arranger's bread and butter. In the hands of even an average player it can enable your group to perform efficiently in a variety of styles. A standard right-handed layout (see Figure 1) will consist of:

- A bass drum, also known as the kick drum, played with the right foot.
- A snare/side drum, played with sticks or brushes.
- A hi-hat foot cymbal, played with a combination of left foot and sticks. It can also be opened and closed and is the standard way for jazz drummers to lightly keep the offbeats 2 and 4 ticking away, leaving the left hand free to do other things.
- A ride cymbal, played with the right-hand stick/brush.

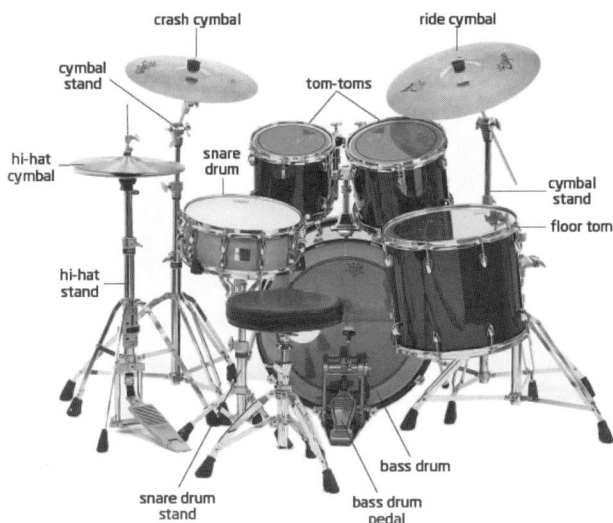

Figure 1:   A standard drum kit

- A crash cymbal, also played with the right-hand stick/brush.
- Up to three tom-toms of varying (indeterminate) pitches: high, middle, low.

In addition to the above, a player might attach further instruments to the basic kit, such as a small splash cymbal, triangle, cowbell or temple block.

HOW TO WRITE FOR DRUM KIT

The cry of 'but I can't write drum parts' is a familiar one for the inexperienced arranger, and it is a great shame as it is really quite simple. The key aspect to bear in mind is this:

No matter what you write in popular music, the player will rarely play it exactly.

This is a salutary lesson to learn very early on, but it is not to criticise your drummer. As an arranger and/or director, you will expect your player to find the groove as accurately as possible and deliver it; whether it be funk, swing, heavy rock, samba, bossa nova or rumba, a decent drummer should know how to do it. Not only that, but they will know how to do it better than you, so let them.

What should I write then?
Let us start with the basic drum map, an explanation of the meaning of the notes on the stave. At its simplest, a drum part uses three lines:

- Bottom space = bass drum
- Second space down = snare/side drum
- Top line, as a cross = cymbal.

Example 1

Possible additional notes:

- Any space other than the two listed above = tom-toms, pitched as desired.

Example 2

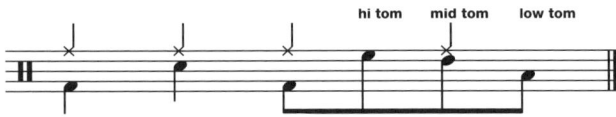

But aren't there several cymbals? How will the player know which one I mean?
You should name them on the part, with clear instructions to switch if required. Thus, you might put:

- To closed hi-hat
- On ride
- To crash
- Cymbal roll.

You might choose to opt for different lines for different cymbals, especially if using software, but this is often unnecessary (and confusing) as far as the player is concerned. Specific written information is preferable.

Example 3

Is it that simple?
Yes, and once you realise that, life becomes so much easier for an arranger. You can tell the player:

- Which sticks to use, for example 'cymbal roll with soft sticks'
- What effect you are looking for: 'gong-like'
- What impact you need: 'build to chorus'.

Example 4

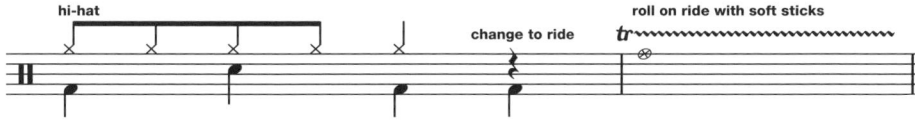

Repetition

Most drum parts are extremely repetitive, and with good reason: you do not want the rhythmic patterns chopping and changing all the time as it is very distracting. Thus you will spend a lot of your time using the repeat bar sign in your music.

However, lines of repeat bars can be tough to follow as it all becomes a blur, so it is nice to give a bit of help. Strategies include:

- **Numbering each bar.** This would be annoying for a constantly active clarinettist, but the drummer will be delighted.
- **Advising what is happening elsewhere in the group.** For instance 'saxophone soli', 'trombone solo', 'full-band/tutti'. This can also provide a strong hint about the associated dynamics required.
- **Providing cues, or even a lead sheet.** Knowing what else is happening in the group and how it affects the drum part can be an enormous asset to the player, so providing the overall melodic line over the top of the drum part can be immensely helpful. It also enables the conductor to discuss the overall arrangement with the player in rehearsal, pointing out which key elements need to be picked out and emphasised. Note the difference between Examples 5b and 5c in terms of how much more sense it makes to the player when the lead part can be followed.

Example 5a

Example 5b

Example 5c (with lead part)

Drum fills

Understandably the writing of drum fills tends to lead to the greatest anxiety of all for the amateur arranger, but once again there is really no need to get stressed. Here is an example of a complex rock fill:

Example 6a

And now, with the right player at the kit, an equally effective way of producing the same result:

Example 6b

The resulting fills are probably going to be slightly different, but they will both do the same lead-in job, and that matters much more than, for instance, which tom-tom is being hit on the 4th semiquaver of beat three. This approach is most effective when the fill is in a gap in the ensemble phrase, meaning there is no requirement to synchronise with any specific rhythmic figure so the drummer is freed up.

How will the player know what I want?
He won't to start with, but he will have a fair idea and may offer plenty of alternatives in rehearsal. Between you you will come up with a satisfying solution

(although he still might not do exactly the same in the performance anyway, depending on how he is feeling at the time and the level of adrenalin flowing).

WRITING FOR THE OTHER PERCUSSION INSTRUMENTS

There is not enough space to even scratch the surface of percussion writing in this book. However, here are some ground rules:

- **Less is more**: percussion is frequently overwritten. Unless you can justify to yourself what a specific instrument is adding to the texture/rhythm, leave it out.
- **Exploit the different sticks and beaters**: not just with drums, but with everything else. A rubber beater on a glockenspiel sounds very different from a wooden one, as does a stick/brush/mallet on a cymbal. Experiment, use your ears, and aim to learn constantly.
- **Percussionists can play more instruments than you think in the same piece**: unlike every other player a percussionist is not tied to one instrument or area on the stage. It is quite common for a timpanist to walk away to play a crucial cymbal crash, and then return to the timps in time for the next entry. Similarly the kit player should be happy to move around if there is time available.

  As a general target – especially if your players are reasonably competent – plan to write for one more player than you actually have. Thus two players should be able to cover three parts, three to four, and so on. Providing you plan your percussion parts, thinking ahead and ensuring that there is enough time for the players to get around the stage, there should be no problem. Just remember, they cannot usually play more than two instruments at the same time!
- **Tuned percussion melodies**: avoid giving complete melodic lines to the xylophone or glockenspiel, especially when they are doubling another instrument. It is far more effective to get them to pick out individual phrases and notes.

Try to be realistic in your demands of your percussionists, by studying scores and parts, talking to players and attending concerts to observe the percussion section at work, and avoid making classic mistakes or producing impossible parts. Even with no more than two players and limited resources at your disposal it is extraordinary what can be achieved, and your arrangements will stand out for their colour and excitement as a result.

PIANO/KEYBOARD WRITING

Just as with percussion, it is impossible to encapsulate the variety of piano writing available to the amateur arranger in this book. However, once again, there are a number of basic strategies which can be employed effectively and with the minimum of fuss. Audio of these examples can be found on the book's companions website.

Example 7: Oom-cha

The oom-cha accompaniment (or oom-pah-pah in 3 time) is surprisingly effective for rhythmic music, such as rock, ska, waltz. Do not dismiss it lightly.

Example 8: Flowing

If your melody is lyrical and flowing, the piano must match it – use quavers, and plenty of broken chords/arpeggios. Note that chords work much better in the high/middle registers than in the bass register. For rock and jazz piano, the right hand will be around about middle C for much of the time.

Example 9: Left-hand octaves

A left-hand single line/doubled in octaves under a right-hand chord will often be very powerful.

Example 10: Both hands in octaves, high

Both hands working in octaves can be very effective, notably in styles such as salsa.

Example 11: Accompaniment above melody

Try the accompaniment above the melody: it does not always have to be below.

Example 12: Piano doubles part of melodic line, not all

Avoid doubling the melody throughout because it becomes tedious, but aim to pick out sections of the melodic line in the piano (rather as with the tuned percussion on page 119).

Melodic interest: remember that the piano can play music other than chord sequences. This fact is often overlooked by beginner arrangers, who associate the keyboard with chords only. Especially with choirs, try to interact and share out the melody between the voices and the piano line.

Example 13: Redundant bass line

If you have access to a bass player, there is no need for the left-hand part to have the bass line all the time (although it may be wise to include optional cue notes for rehearsal purposes). The additional bass will allow you to voice the piano part in a more appropriate two-hand style, aiming to avoid the root of the chord as the lowest note.

Example 13a: Bass line in left hand in absence of bass player

Example 13b: Bass line cued in piano but not played, enabling improved piano voicings

There will be an opportunity to explore some further aspects of piano writing in Chapters 10 and 11.

HARMONY AND HARMONISATION

This is another aspect of arranging which can cause concern, yet while it is undeniable that harmonic skills are a key part of the arranger's armoury, it is surprising how few chords are needed at a basic level.

For folk songs or rock it is often preferable to keep it as simple as possible, reserving more complex chords for jazz and gospel. As a rule, you can probably manage very well with just the following:

- Primary chords: I, IV and V(7), in root position and 1st inversions
- Secondary chords: II and VI
- Cadences: perfect, imperfect, occasionally interrupted
- Simple extensions: 7ths and 9ths
- Pedal/inverted pedals, either dominant or tonic: these can be sustained or repeated.

The above will get you a long way, certainly at the start.

Modulation: to change key or not?

There is one question to be asked when it comes to changing key:

Am I just changing key for the sake of it, or is there a reason?

Three supplementary questions follow:

- When, and how often? Should it just be near the end, or maybe earlier in the piece? Should there be more than one key change?
- How do I go about it?
- To which key?

Unless there is a satisfactory answer to the first question the others don't even come into the equation. Successful, effective modulation should be done for a purpose.

So what reasons might there be?
- **Variety:** we have been in the same key long enough and need a change. Five verses in C major can get rather wearing.
- **Practicality:** there may be issues with voice ranges (in the case of a proposed descant, for example) or with instrument choice because you want to use a flute next, but the notes will be too low unless you change key. You will also need to consider writing idiomatically as the music, which is currently in a sharp key (G major), is great for strings but not ideal for the saxophones who are about to play next and would prefer a flat key (B♭/E♭/A♭ major).
- **Emotional impact:** as every *X Factor* arranger knows, raising the key will raise the temperature of the audience.

Which key should I go to?
Aim to stick to the standard key relationships for now:

- **Dominant/V:** ideal for a more optimistic, brighter feel
- **Subdominant/IV:** produces a more mellow, relaxed mood

- **Relative/VI or Tonic/I minors:** you are unlikely to change mode in a cover version approach, but you will certainly need the major/minor option in a theme and variations.

There are a couple of other keys available:

- **Up the tone/semitone:** as discussed above, the clichéd 'getting up from the stool and walking forward' moment. It is certainly not new; witness the ruthlessness with which Leonard Bernstein satirises this vaudeville technique throughout 'Officer Krupke' from *West Side Story*.
- **The flattened submediant** ($\flat$VI): trickier to do (see below), but a lovely effect when it works.

How to modulate

Changing key is actually a much easier process than it looks. It all hinges around the idea of the perfect cadence. In essence what you need to do is create a perfect cadence in the new key, that is the key you are modulating to. So, for example, C major to G major (tonic to dominant) requires a perfect cadence in G major, ideally with three chords:

IV – V – I (C – D – G)

II – V – I (Am – D – G)

Example 14a: Perfect cadence 1

IV(C)   V⁷(D⁷)   I(G)

Example 14b: Perfect cadence 2

IIb(Am)   V⁷(D⁷)   I(G)

These are the best two options, and the equivalent Roman numerals work in any key. The appearance of D major provides the required F♯, but it is the cadence (not just the accidental) which establishes the new key. Note that chord V is *always* major in tonal music.

In all cases you will end up with a *pivot chord*, that is a chord that features in both the current key *and* the target key, for example, G major to D major: G is chord I in G, but chord IV in D.

Other modulation techniques

Example 15: Via a sequence

You may need to adjust the melody slightly, possibly adding/subtracting accidentals, and then stop when you reach the key you want.

Example 16: Via a diminished 7th chord

This ambiguous chord, constructed from minor 3rds, is not in a key so can resolve to anywhere.

Dim7th   V⁷   I

Example 17: Out of silence

The ear loses track of the original key and accepts the new one. This works very well in a resonant acoustic, enabling the previous chord to die away of its own accord before the new key enters.

Example 18: After a lengthy drum solo

The above technique can also work after **a fill/section for drums/unpitched percussion**. Provided there are no recognisable pitches the ear will soon lose track of the prevailing harmony and gladly accept the next key that arrives.

Example 19: The suspended note

Here the role of a specific note changes from one chord to the next. We might call this a pivot note, as it functions in very much the same way as a pivot chord. Thus C is the tonic of C major but, especially when sustained hanging on its own without an accompaniment for several beats, that C can then be reharmonised as the fifth of F major, or even the major 7th of D♭ major. Further explanation and audio examples of this technique can be found on the companion website to this book.

And so to the arrangement itself ...

THE BASIC FOUR

In general, most simple arranging is always concerned with four elements:

- Melody
- Accompaniment/harmony
- Bass line
- Rhythm.

It is the need to balance and vary these four aspects that makes arranging so fascinating but also challenging, and it takes time and practice to get it right.

Melody

This is not just the tune, but everything associated with the melodic line:

- **Unisons/octaves:** both for colour and balance/strength
- **The thickened line:** how the melody is harmonised – 3rds, 6ths, 4ths – and what effect that has on the listener
- **Countermelody and descant:** both need to interact closely with the original melodic line.

Accompaniment/harmony

This is everything supporting the melodic line at that moment. It involves:

- **Harmony:** anything from basic primary I, IV and V right through to extended chords such as 11ths and 13ths
- **Rhythmic ostinati/riffs:** repetitive inner ideas which create the rhythmic drive
- **Accompaniment style:** smooth or spiky, dissonant or pleasing, driving forward or relaxed.

Bass line and rhythm

These last two elements, especially in popular music styles, influence and dictate the overall feel of the piece. Get them wrong and the music does not work. These include aspects such as:

- **Authentic bass lines:** it is the bass line (not the drums) that creates the style/genre, and that is what makes it so important. Whatever it is – blues, hip hop, gospel, swing, reggae, funk, samba – the bass line will usually define it.

- **Drums and percussion**: as discussed above, even if the bass line has already done much of the work in creating the style, it still needs the percussion to add the requisite colour and drive.

Naturally, as with all creative work, the above elements cannot be treated in isolation, nor should they be. A punchy melody will need an equally punchy accompaniment and bass line if it is to function properly. There may also be opportunities for deliberately contrasting lines to provide variety and intentional incongruity.

However, as a beginner, it is not a bad approach to consider the following questions at any point in the arrangement:

- What style is this?
- Who has the tune at the moment?
- Who has the accompaniment?
- What percussion/rhythm do I need?

THE PLAN

Let us use a cooking analogy here. You have all the available ingredients laid out for you, you understand the flavours of each and how they might work together in combination, and you know that you can use each one as sparingly or as lavishly as you wish. Now you need to create your recipe.

Before you start to write your arrangement you should really have a plan. For a straightforward pop song you might have:

Structure: Intro – Verse 1 – Chorus – Verse 2 – Chorus – Instrumental – Chorus – Ending
Instrumentation: SA/men choir, piano, bass, drums, (percussion)

Here your thought processes might work like this, although not necessarily chronologically at this stage:

- I'll start with just piano, and bring the drums in halfway through
- I'll use the final phrase of the tune for the intro
- I'll probably start with unison voices, or maybe a solo
- I might consider changing key for the last chorus – might also add a tambourine
- I'll make sure I have a powerful, push-button ending – this will probably go at the end of the first half of the concert.

There is quite a bit here, plenty of detail, and an understanding of the emotional shape and the effect it will have on the audience. It is not all finalised, but that does not matter, you are certainly in a position to start now. Of course, the plan may change once you get going, but at least you've avoided the blank-page syndrome.

Should I use computer software?
In many ways this depends on how confident you are with computers, but there are many benefits, not least that it enables you to hear back what you have just written. It may not matter quite so much for a small choir/piano set-up, but when arranging for a wind band – in full transposed score – few of us possess the score-reading skills required to perform the numerous parts.

Another major bonus is the fact that most notation software programmes possess similar functions to a word processor – copy, paste, delete, insert – which can be very useful when you are deciding who is to play what. It only takes a moment to copy the flute part into the clarinet part, delete or rewrite the flute part, and the clarinet has the tune.

Lastly, it will enable you to print out decent, professional-looking sheet music to give to your members, and the automatic appearance of bar numbers and/ or rehearsal letters in your score will certainly make your rehearsals smoother and more efficient.

So is software a good thing?
Provided you research it well and get what you need, being careful not to purchase sequencing software which rarely offers convincing notation, then computer software is to be recommended if you can afford it. But it may not be right for you, in which case there is absolutely nothing wrong with old-fashioned pencil and manuscript if that makes you feel more comfortable. What matters is the resulting music, and providing your handwritten notation is legible and of a suitable size, that is fine.

In Part V of this book, the final two chapters will look in detail at two arrangement Case Studies: one choral, one instrumental. These studies will provide examples and strategies as to how to approach arranging a specific song.

PART V:
CHORAL AND INSTRUMENTAL ARRANGEMENT CASE STUDIES

In this chapter we will look at various approaches to a specific song, exploring the possibilities open to the choral arranger and suggesting some ideas and strategies. Audio of these examples can be found on the book's companion website.

The piece we are going to use is just one of many versions of a well-known folk song, originally English before being transported to the Appalachian Mountains of North America. The much-recorded song 'The Twelfth of Never' is also based on this melody and lyric but, unlike the public-domain version below, that song is classed as being *adapted* (by Jerry Livingston and Paul Francis Webster) and is thus very much still in copyright.

I Gave My Love a Cherry (The Riddle Song): Traditional

I gave my love a cherry that had no stone
I gave my love a chicken that had no bone
I gave my love a story that had no end
I gave my love a baby with no cryin'

How can there be a cherry which has no stone?
How can there be a chicken which has no bone?
How can there be a story which has no end?
How can there be a baby with no cryin'?

A cherry when it's blooming, it has no stone
A chicken when it's pippin, it has no bone
The story that I love you, it has no end
A baby when it's sleeping, has no cryin'

There are numerous theories as to the meaning behind the song, some more convincing than others, so it is probably best just to treat it as the evocative lullaby it was intended to be.

The structure is **strophic**, in that the same melody is used for all three verses, and the song lends itself to an atmospheric and haunting setting, enabling the arranger to experiment with some unusual harmonies while maintaining the innate simplicity. It is also relatively short, with the story arc being completed in just three four-line verses.

PART 1: HARMONISING THE MELODY

If you are experienced in this aspect, you may wish to skip to the section on page 141, which deals with part writing.

It is quite possible that the tune you choose will already have its own associated **chord sequence**, in which case there is no need to devise your own. However, all good arrangers should check the given sequence and, if necessary, alter some chords to provide variety.

Before any sort of arranging it is essential that you know the **harmonic structure** of the tune at its basic level: the **primary chords** I (tonic), IV (subdominant) and V (dominant).

Roman numerals

Chords expressed as Roman numerals refer to the numbered notes in the scale, and are generally more useful than simple letter names as they are transferable, that is they can be applied in any key. You should always aim to think in these terms if at all possible, as it makes any subsequent **transposition** much easier.

Thus, in this example: F major (I), Bb major (IV) and C major (V).

Most simple tunes will work with just these three chords, although you will need more in due course.

Example 1: Primary root position chords

This is the most basic harmonisation of this tune, and it should not be dismissed too quickly. A traditional folk tune may not sit well with too much complex harmony and you may find yourself opting for simplicity, especially early on.

Root position chords will inevitably result in jumpy bass lines. This is fine at **cadences**, but not so good elsewhere. The bass line can be smoothed out in a number of ways, with the use of:

- **Inversions:** choose a note of the chord *other than the root* in the bass line. Thus in bar 3 we use a B♭ chord over a D bass – the chord is still clear, but slightly softened in its impact.
- **Passing notes:** in the same bar there is an opportunity for a rising passing note into the next bar, which also helps the line.
- **Contrary motion:** the bass line in bars 3 and 4 is moving in the *opposite direction* to the melody. This is ideal and should be done as much as possible, especially if the tune is going high, as it acoustically balances out the rising melodic line.
- **Scalic bass lines:** these will always give a piece strength and direction, and allow us to explore the different qualities of the various inversions.
- **Dominant 7ths:** chord V is the standard set-up chord for a **perfect cadence** at the end of a phrase, but always test out the V7 as well, as the 7th note has an even more powerful pushing effect into the subsequent tonic chord.

Example 2: Inversions, passing notes and dominant 7ths

There is no need for the bass line to move all the time. It is often just as effective to shift the chords over a single **pedal note** (which can be sustained or repeated).

Sometimes this approach can result in weak or unstable chords, notably second inversions with the 5th of the chord as the bass (for instance, in bar 6). However, provided the pedal lasts for several bars the ear will factor this in and treat the bass note as a pedal rather than part of the chord.

Example 3a: Pedal notes

Should you have access to a keyboard or organ rather than a piano (that is to say an instrument which offers a *sustaining timbre*), you should also experiment with the **inverted pedal** where the pedal note is *above* the melodic line at the top of the texture. In this case the dominant (5th) of the chord is often the best option, and the resulting temporary gentle clashes with the tune can be very effective.

Example 3b: Inverted pedal notes

Secondary chords and harmonic substitution

Replacing primary chords with more adventurous and less predictable harmony is a key part of the arranger's art, as such chords can provide variety and changes in mood. In addition they offer some welcome minor inflections in an otherwise major mode. In general, the following should work due to the notes in common between the two chords:

- I/F can be replaced with VI/D minor (**submediant**)
- IV/B♭ can be replaced with II/G minor (**supertonic**)
- V(7) can also be substituted, but be wary: it is often wise to *keep it as the original* (perhaps with an inversion) as it is such a powerful chord already.

Example 4: Adding secondary chords and harmonic substitution

I gave my love a cher-ry that had no stone, I gave my love a chick-en that had no bone, I

Ib   IV   II   I   V⁷   VI⁷   III   V

gave my love a sto-ry that had no end, I gave my love a ba-by with no cry-ing.

V⁷   I   VI⁷   V⁷   IV   II   IV/C   I

Substitution is great fun, but handle with care. In tonal music the tonic is crucial for establishing key and should not be dismissed. This is especially true at the start and end of the tune, unless you are deliberately aiming for ambiguity (perhaps as a response to the text).

Extended chords and internal modulations

Once you become more confident with primary and secondary chords, you may want to experiment with the more daring aspects of harmony. These include **extension chords** (7ths, 9ths and 11ths) as well as **diminished** and **augmented** harmony.

You might also attempt some **internal modulations** such as the changes to B♭ major and D minor in this example. Note the deliberate injection of the perfect cadence in the key we are approaching: II – V7 – I in B♭ major in bars 8–9, and V7 – I in D minor between bars 9 and 10. These all add new colour and shape to the music, and change the impact of the unaltered tune.

As this piece is originally a traditional song it is tempting to add a **modal** element into the mix – the major 9th chord on the flattened 7th in bar 15 is unexpected, and yet strangely seems to fit with the folk song idiom.

Example 5: Extended chords and modulations

The power of harmony

As an arranger you should never give up the quest for new colours and ideas. Harmony is such a powerful tool and can significantly enhance the impact of your melody. Resist the temptation to play safe, as it will limit you and your singers in the long run. As composer Sarah Shaw says, on writing music for young people:

'It is vital that the harmony contributes more to the song than just a basic support of the melodic line. Introducing different moods invoked by added sixths, flattened, augmented or diminished chords and more complex modulations ... expands the emotional vocabulary enormously, imperceptibly developing the range of musical experience.'

(*Music Teacher*, May 2009)

Changing key

As discussed in Chapter 9, you should never change key for the sake of it, but you should always know how to go about it. Modulation is an essential tool for the arranger.

Modulation to the subdominant

By adding an extra bar to the phrases, during which you create a II (Cm) – V7 (F7) – I (Bb) cadence, it is relatively easy to modulate to Bb major. This is most likely to appear in the final verse, where the change in register will send the soprano line up to a high F (with the tantalising possibility of a top Bb descant if desired).

The intentional omission of the 3rd (E) in the C7 chord prevents any sense of a jarring **false relation** – two different versions of the same note in close proximity – when the Eb appears in the next bar.

Example 6a: Modulation to the subdominant (Bb major)

Modulation to the dominant

This is trickier, necessitating an alteration to the last note of the original melody, but the principle is still the same: II (Dm) – V7 (G7) – I (C), with a B♮ being introduced into the descending scale under the D minor chord. As this is a less natural change than the one to the subdominant it is wise to develop a new melody in the top line of the piano which leads nicely to the G, setting up the note for the new entry.

Example 6b: Modulation to the dominant (C major)

The above is just an overview of what you might do with harmonies in your choral arranging. There are many more options, and so many different ways of harmonising the same note, as demonstrated below.

Example 6c: Alternative treatments of one note – C

As usual there are no right or wrong answers. It all comes down to four elements:

- **Your ears:** do you like what you hear and does it make harmonic sense?
- **The audience:** who are they, and what are they likely to expect from you and your choir?
- **The performance location:** complex harmonies may be approved of at a music festival, but may not be quite so popular at a wedding or school fete.
- **Your choir:** how capable are they of doing justice to what you have written? Will the carefully planned dissonances be effective in performance, or just sound wrong?

There is no need to toe the line – you may have a strong desire to stretch your singers and perhaps they need it at this stage in the group's development. However, be aware of the impact your arrangement might have, especially if it is adventurous, and be prepared for constructive criticism. Whatever you do, don't give up. All arranging is a learning curve, so persevere.

PART 2: PART WRITING

Whatever harmonisation you opt for, you now need to decide how to share out and thicken the melodic line. You must also consider issues of accompaniment, rhythmic interest, countermelodies and descants, and effective piano parts.

Example 7a: Unisons and octaves

The use of **unison** is to be highly recommended, especially with inexperienced choirs, and is a convincing way of starting a piece when everyone is nervous – the 'safety in numbers' element is very powerful.

In this example the alto voice colour will predominate at the start, as this range is low for sopranos (although they should still sing). The second phrase is more suited to male voices than the first, as it is clearly in the baritone range. Notice the optional solo here – write the line for everyone, but be willing to try one or two soloists to change the colours as every voice in your choir will be different.

Example 7b: Humming

Whether or not you choose to have a piano accompaniment, humming is always effective choral writing. Notice also the change to the warmer 'aah' sound over the second phrase.

Example 8: Parallel 3rds and 6ths

As the Everly Brothers, The Beatles and many others have proved, harmonising in parallel 3rds usually works very well for simple tunes. In this instance every chord fits (Example 8a). The parallel 6ths, however, do not work quite so perfectly here (Example 8b), and a few adaptations are required in order to maintain the link with the chord structure. The line is also above the melody, so you must be certain that the alto tune will cut through (perhaps by adding a tenor if you have one).

Example 8a: Parallel 3rds

Example 8b: Parallel 6ths above melody, with adaptions

Example 9: Harmony out of unison

Close harmony **dissonance** can be difficult for inexperienced singers, as many will instinctively gravitate to the melodic line rather than go against it. The solution is to start the line in unison and then move one of the parts by step while holding the other. The resulting 2nds are suitably piquant, and nobody feels intimidated.

The same applies to **suspensions**, such as in bars 4 and 8 below. It is much easier to clash when it is the same note as you were singing previously, and the downward **resolution** is the only logical way to go.

Handled carefully you can use a surprising amount of dissonance in your arranging, especially when the text calls for it – words such as 'pain', death' and 'agony' spring to mind. Dissonance is a powerful harmonic shorthand for expressing emotion.

Example 10: Three-part chords

Putting the three lines together is relatively simple provided you follow the given chords, although you must be a little bit wary of the male voices overpowering the sopranos and altos, especially when the latter parts are low in their ranges. In this instance the second phrase will work better than the first. As top West End arranger David Cullen explains:

'In terms of balance it is generally the tenor part that needs most consideration ... try to make it pleasing and melodic in its own right. Be aware of how the sound of amateur tenors can brighten as you pass E, and in general save the high register for forte passages.'

(personal communication with author via email)

Notice that the lowest vocal line does not always have the root of the chord, and instead has several **second inversions**: the piano provides the true bass. The movement is generally in **parallel**, but as the soprano rises in bar 6 **contrary motion** is much more desirable. The final beat of bar 5 also produces a problem. Exact parallel/similar motion would result in consecutive 5ths, so an adjustment is made to avoid this part-writing 'crime'.

It may seem strange to be worried about 'correct' part writing in the 21st century – surely ancient rules such as avoiding parallel 5ths, not doubling the 3rd in major chords and preparing and resolving dissonances properly are passé by now? And yet it is extraordinary how well these rules still work in practice, producing satisfying harmonisations and voice leading as a result. By all means break the rules if you wish, but always be aware of the implications of doing so and, in general, don't dismiss Bach's ideas just yet.

All parts move homophonically (in chords), but there is still scope for the occasional passing note, such as on the 4th beat of bar 7. The flowing piano part should help to counteract any potential stodginess in the block chord writing.

Example 11: Inner part writing

Even when primary harmony is deemed appropriate for your needs there will still be a danger that it may become overly predictable. However, your instinct to reach for substitute chords and complex harmonies should be curbed, as there may be another way to solve the problem: moving the inner parts. Not only can this create rhythmic interest, it can also add much-needed spice and colour to a simple chord structure.

'Moving an inner voice of a chord is a good way to provide interest and prevent a passage from becoming static.'

(Sebesky, 1994)

'Look after the inner parts and try to make them melodic in their own right: where possible bring each part back after some chromatic movement to notes they held before: and compensate a descending phrase with a rising one.'

(David Cullen, personal communication with author via email)

Maintaining and developing the interest levels

Throughout each of the above approaches all the parts are moving together and everything is dictated by the shape and rhythm of the original tune. Now we need to start exploring ways of separating the lines and developing the various melodic and rhythmic ideas. For this we will need to create new musical lines and **motifs** which interlock with the original material but also offer welcome freshness.

Example 12: Descants and countermelodies

Looking back at Example 8b it could be argued that the line created by the parallel 6ths is acting as a form of **descant** because it is above the melody.

However, both parts are moving simultaneously, so really this is just a thickened line. A true descant is a separate line which interlocks with the original tune.

What is the difference between a descant and a countermelody?
Aside from the fact that a descant is above the tune, whereas a **countermelody** could be anywhere in the texture, this is a tricky question. The simplest way of thinking about it – although by no means a definition – is that a descant requires its associated tune to work properly, whereas a true countermelody should be able to exist on its own. A fuller explanation of the difference between the two approaches is available on the book's companion website.

How does this influence my approach to writing and arranging?
You should always attempt to create a strong, self-sufficient tune with every countermelody or descant you devise. Be proud of your creation. Your new tune should have its own individual character, perhaps by using different rhythms or entering unexpectedly. You might also try to carry part of your new phrase over the conventional periodic phrasing (balanced 2s, 4s or 8s) of the theme.

Example 12a: Descant with different rhythms and words

Example 12b: Descant with countermelody

FURTHER APPROACHES

In addition to the choral writing, it is important to consider other aspects, notably the accompaniment or otherwise. Some possible approaches:

- **A cappella**: completely unaccompanied. This is much tougher than it looks, both for the arranger and for the singers. Not only is it very exposed, but you will also need to develop the skill of *implied* harmonies where you do not have enough voices to create the full chord. This is especially true of S(S)A choirs where you have no effective way of producing a bass line. You may well end up writing a cappella in the future, but it is not a wise place to start. However, if you have a confident soloist who is capable of staying in tune, a brief unaccompanied section might work very well.
- **Accompanied** by keyboard/guitar. This is the easiest and most obvious approach. The additional chordal instrument can double the melody, fill in any missing harmonies and create bass lines. There is also scope for keyboards other than piano, such as organ or synthesiser, to produce different instrumental colours. A modern electronic keyboard will also be able to evoke the sound of a particular popular music era, such as the 1980s.

- **Additional bass and drums:** once you know how to write for drums (see Chapter 9) the addition of a drum kit can have a major impact in rock or jazz repertoire and is to be highly recommended. Similarly a bass (guitar or string) might appear to be simply doubling the left-hand piano part, but there is no substitute for the real thing, notably in jazz or funk.

- **Additional percussion:** especially in Latin-American, Caribbean or African music, where the extra colour is both evocative and rhythmic. Extra percussion does not have to be complex to be effective, and can even be performed by members of the choir while they are singing, and the visual impact of such an approach should not be underestimated.

Further examples of more complex independent part-writing and piano accompaniments can be found on the book's companion website.

VOCAL RANGES

The voice is a surprisingly flexible instrument, and each voice can often sing another's part. Thus an alto can sing a tenor line or a soprano line, and a bass can sing tenor if required – they are effectively interchangeable. However, while an alto singer *can* sing a soprano line, she won't really want to because it will feel quite high, and vice versa – a soprano *can* sing lower, but not terribly well, and the voice will not really have the quality of either an alto or soprano, but will be somewhere in between.

Voice quality is key here. A rich baritone timbre is not the same as a middle-range tenor, even when they are singing the same note. Similarly a soprano's middle C does not sound the same as an alto's middle C.

Think of effective vocal ranges as being where the various voices *work best* and *enjoy singing*: high sopranos and tenors, low basses and altos. There are no rules as such and every choir and voice is different, but it is a good start.

The various techniques and approaches outlined above are just a sample of the possibilities open to the choral arranger. All may work in various contexts, and none will work absolutely everywhere. It is up to you and your personal taste, there is no definitive correct way, and that is the thrill of arranging.

For a complete SATB/piano arrangement of 'I Gave My Love a Cherry', please visit the companion website where you will find a version available to download and use with your choir.

LCHORALSTYLESARRANGING
ANNINGVENUEVOCALSDYNAMICS
ONDUCTINGADMINISTRATION
VENUESOUNDDYNAMICSMANAGING
PTEACHINGCONDUCTINGLI
ORMANCEPRACTICALITIES
TINGS
ENUEDYNAMICSMANAGINGCHORAL
RCUSSIONINSTRUMENTA
LIGHTINGSCORINGSTYLES

CHAPTER 11:
INSTRUMENTAL ARRANGEMENT
— THEME AND VARIATIONS

In this chapter we are going to look at devising an instrumental arrangement based on the tune 'Daisy Bell'. We will explore the use of instrumentation and pastiche, including the importance of modelling, leading to a number of possible variation openings in a range of classical and popular styles.

The structure of theme and variations has long been a favoured form with composers, and it is a good starting point for the beginner arranger. It offers the perfect combination for the listener: repetition and contrast. The tune is always present in some recognisable form but is frequently disguised. It also encourages the arranger to explore a variety of styles of music, both classical and popular, and can often result in a satisfying overall result.

The steps involved are:

- Select your theme
- Analyse your theme
- Harmonise your theme
- Experiment with various dance styles
- Organise your variations into a satisfying order
- Define your instrumentation
- Write a draft version
- Try it with your players
- Rewrite and retry
- Perform.

THE THEME

In the future you may want to compose your own theme, but for the moment let us start with something which is well known and in the public domain. There are numerous examples to choose from – nursery rhymes are good, as are Christmas carols. Here we have chosen a song from the Old Time Music Hall, 'Daisy Bell', composed by Harry Dacre in 1892:

> Daisy, daisy, give me your answer do
> I'm half crazy, all for the love of you
> It won't be a stylish marriage,
> I can't afford a carriage
> But you'll look sweet upon the seat
> Of a bicycle made for two.

As this is going to be a purely instrumental arrangement we can ignore the words to a certain extent. This will actually be very freeing, as the need for words and rhythms to make sense in choral writing can often limit what the arranger would like to do with the tune. Now there are no such strictures, and we can treat the song as pure melody.

However, there may still be a little bit of scope for humour and reference to the word 'marriage' – snippets of Mendelssohn and Wagner wedding marches may well creep in at some point.

Example 1: The melody

Example 1 shows the melody clearly divided into four sections: A, A1, B, C. There are also a few smaller ideas (or **motifs**) which may be used in isolation, perhaps as **ostinati** (repeated ideas), marked x, y, z.

Defining the structure of the tune is very important, as it allows us to analyse the various sections and decide which ones to use and when. For example, introductions may not always start with A, perhaps opting for C instead (which naturally leads into the start of the next verse). Or B, with its repetitive nature, may end up as an accompaniment or backing figure at some point.

Example 2: Ostinato

All we are doing at this stage is breaking up the full melody into shorter sections and spotting ideas – melodic and rhythmic – which may or may not appear in the full arrangement. It does not matter where or how at the moment, but we always need to have these ideas in the back of our mind.

ORGANIC DEVELOPMENT

In order to unify the whole work, it is important that we use *as few new ideas as possible*. In an ideal world, all the musical material will be derived in some way from the original melody.

'When the need is felt for a fresh melodic statement, it's advisable to try a variation on a motive already used before injecting a new one.'

(Sebesky, 1994)

This can be challenging, but it does result in a sense that all the variations are strongly linked other than by the original tune.

Harmonising the tune

Before starting to arrange, even if you already have plenty of ideas buzzing around your head, it is essential that you produce a straightforward harmonisation of the theme. It is quite possible that the tune you choose will already have its own associated **chord sequence**, in which case there is no need to devise your own. However, all good arrangers should check the given sequence and, if necessary, alter some chords to provide variety.

We start, as always, with the **primary chords**: I, IV and V. Most simple tonal (major/minor) tunes can be harmonised in this way, and this tune is no exception (Example 3).

Roman numerals

Chords expressed as Roman numerals refer to the numbered notes in the scale, and are generally more useful than simple letter names as the former are transferable, that is to say they can be applied in any key. You should always aim to think in these terms if at all possible, as it makes any subsequent **transposition** much easier.

Thus, in F major, we will just use the chords of F, B♭ and C. We choose the chords by a combination of theory (which chord fits the given melody note best) and ear (which of the three sounds right to us). At this early stage there are few options open to us, although there is an unexpected twist halfway through which needs to be addressed.

Internal modulation

Most simple tunes remain in the same key throughout, but 'Daisy Bell' is an exception, as it **modulates** to C major (the dominant or fifth) at the end of bar 16. However, this is only a short-lived detour – we are soon back in F major again – and it is managed easily enough via a brief perfect cadence (V-I) in the new key. (The carol 'Away in a Manger' does exactly the same.) This pleasant diversion is part of the song's overall charm, but there is no need for alarm. As we shall see, changing key is much simpler than it looks.

Example 3: Primary chords

Adding secondary harmony

The use of chords I, IV and V with such a simple melody will work fine throughout the piece, but it would be a shame to limit ourselves: half the fun of arranging is devising new chords to fit the melody (Example 4).

As we shall see there are many options available to us, many of them related to the style chosen, but for the moment we will concentrate on the **substitution** of **secondary** chords, plus the dominant 7th. Thus chord V will become V7, adding a bit of colour to the straightforward triad.

Substitute chords

Wherever we originally selected chord I (F), this can often be substituted with chord VI (D minor). The same applies to chord IV (B♭), which may be switched to chord II (G minor). This injection of minor tonality will be much needed at points, as purely major tonality can be wearing after a while.

However, substitute chords must be handled with care, as it is not just a mathematical exercise. Chord VI would fit bar 1, for example, but the ear would be confused into thinking that the whole tune was in a minor key and the overall effect would be ambiguous – fine for halfway through the work perhaps, but not at the start. Similarly, the brief internal modulation (bar 16) referred to above is already harmonically interesting and does not need further changes.

Overall, our aim in this harmonisation is to keep the basic major quality of the tune intact while adding some minor colour at certain points.

Example 4: Secondary chords

A simple piano part

Once we have worked out a satisfactory harmonisation/chord sequence it is time to devise a simple piano part from which to work (guitarists may prefer to work it out on their instrument, of course, but the principle is the same). As this tune is clearly a gentle waltz, a straightforward oompah-pah pattern will more than suffice at this stage. This does not mean that all the ensuing variations will be in 3 time – far from it – but we need to start from the original (Example 5).

Note the unexpected use of chord III in bar 2, and the use of **inversions** to produce **scalic bass lines**. Note also how the **harmonic rhythm** – the speed at which the chords change – increases towards the cadence.

The overall harmonisation is enhanced by a simple thickening of the melodic line, mostly using intervals of 3rds and 6ths (with occasional 4ths to fit the prevailing harmony).

Example 5: Simple accompaniment

We now have the basics: a decent, well-structured and analysed theme, effectively and sensibly harmonised.

The arrangement itself

Unless you are very confident, you will not try to be too original in your first attempts at variations. Not only is there nothing wrong with this conservative approach but, more importantly, it is eminently advisable. Composers through the years have learned from each other, and it is perfectly acceptable to compose in another person's style. Hollywood composers have been doing it for years, and continue to do so – indeed, that was (and is) their job, with directors frequently requesting Straussian waltzes or Sousa-like marches.

THE ART OF COMMERCIAL PASTICHE

The world of musical theatre is full of **pastiche** (the art of making your music sound like someone else's). Both *Grease* and *Hairspray* are deliberately written in pop styles (1950s and 1960s respectively) which evoke past eras, as is Alan Menken's 1970s' soul/disco score for *Sister Act: The Musical*. The idea is not new: Sandy Wilson's *The Boy Friend* evokes the Charleston era of the 1920s, despite being written thirty years after. All successful Hollywood composers have had to learn how to write like Tchaikovsky, Handel or Shostakovich, and they sometimes even need to sound like their predecessors. One such example is John Williams channelling the Viennese romanticism brought to the USA by Korngold and Steiner. And, in addition to *Hairspray*, composer Marc Shaiman's score for the Doris Day/Rock Hudson homage *Down With Love* brilliantly evokes the film music of the early 1960s.

Away from America, consider the work of composer Eric Rogers for the *Carry On* films. His swing version of 'One Man Went to Mow' for the opening titles of *Carry On Camping*, and the different versions of 'Oh Dear, What Can the Matter Be?' for *Carry On at Your Convenience*, for example, are great fun and beautifully done. For more educational amusement, try *Bill Bailey's Remarkable Guide to the Orchestra*, featuring composer Anne Dudley's masterly pastiche of US 1970s' cop show incidental music.

So how does this affect my arranging? I cannot be expected to know all this music, surely, and I certainly cannot write like Tchaikovsky or John Williams ... No, but you can start to learn and you can *listen*. The key is this: there is no need for your arrangements to sound exactly like Tchaikovsky, but your aim is to create a reaction from your listener along the lines of 'that sounds a bit like *Swan Lake*'. That's all, nothing more.

And no, of course you cannot be expected to know a vast amount of music, but you can at least try to extend your musical knowledge.

'...the more music you are aware of, the better equipped you will be ... Learn to keep your ears and your mind open.'

(Sebesky, 1994)

Commercial pastiche is not about sounding exactly like a style but getting a sense of it, creating an *impression*. There is no great need for authenticity. In order to arrange in the style of an authentic Argentinian tango, for example, you would need to study the music in detail, but your audience does not expect it. Far better to listen to the pastiche tango of 'Hernando's Hideaway' (from Adler and Ross's *The Pajama Game*) or the popular song 'Temptation', and try to imitate that instead.

But this isn't creative, surely?
These are early days in your arranging career and you need to start slowly and relatively safely. There will be plenty of time for experimentation and originality later on. The priority at the moment is to learn the basics and produce decent, entertaining music which people will want to hear. The more you arrange and your confidence grows, the more your own ideas will shine through, but you have to start somewhere. In the words of the eminent jazz writer Sammy Nestico:

'What happens is you pick out four or five favourite writers and emulate them. Little by little, these little pieces of these writers become you.'

(Quoted in Wright, 1983)

The importance of modelling

Before attempting to write a set of variations, the first thing to do is to listen to plenty of examples in varying styles. So what are you listening for?

- How is the theme used in each variation? Is it complete or in sections?
- Are the variations separated or linked together (or is there a mixture)? How is it done and why?
- Can you detect any rules/key approaches regarding the order of the variations, or do they seem randomly put together?
- How are the instruments used, and what effect does it have on the listener?
- Is there a wide variety of moods, or is it all the same?

This sounds like homework to me ...
Don't panic! Music you have known for ages will take on a new life when you start to analyse it as a prospective instrumental arranger, and you will undoubtedly hear things you have never noticed before. It is entirely up to you how much detail you go into, anything from just listening in the car to making

detailed notes while following a score, but it will all help. At this point you are not interested in the style/genre, just the variation techniques being used and how the whole piece is put together.

What to listen to

Theme and variations is one of the most widely used forms in classical music, and that has extended into popular music as well. There are numerous examples, and they will all help in some way. Some suggestions:

- Paganini variations. Try comparing Rachmaninov's *Rhapsody on a Theme of Paganini* with Andrew Lloyd Webber's variations on the same theme
- Bach's *Goldberg Variations*
- Schubert's finale of the *Trout Quintet*
- Brahms' *Variations on a Theme of Haydn*
- Elgar's *Enigma Variations*
- Mozart's 'Ah, Vous Dirai-je, Maman' for piano ('Twinkle, Twinkle Little Star')
- John Dankworth's 'Experiments with Mice', a mini masterclass in pastiche writing of the various big-band genres
- The National Youth Jazz Orchestra's *Big Band Christmas* albums exemplify just what imaginative writers can do with simple carols
- Fred Astaire/Ginger Rogers' films: once the initial vocal is over, listen to the way the dance arrangers spin the tune through various styles. The same is true of Gene Kelly's films such as *Singin' in the Rain* and *An American in Paris*.

There are numerous other examples, such as the chaconne (ground bass) from Gustav Holst's *First Suite for Military Band*, where the composer weaves a set of variations over and around a repeating bass line.

Some of the above may act as a model for your own variations, both in terms of what happens to the theme and the order in which the variations appear.

DANCE FORMS, NATIONAL IDENTITIES AND MARCH STYLES

Dances, national styles and marches are, and have always been, the bread and butter for instrumental arrangers. Each one is instantly recognisable and already has an innate rhythm to it which helps the variation to flow naturally.

They won't all work for every theme, but it is always wise to have them in the back of your mind and not to dismiss them too early. You will be surprised what can happen as the arrangement progresses.

The six categories are:

- **Military:** marches and fanfares
- **Formal/classical:** minuet, gavotte, sarabande, waltz, gigue
- **Nationalistic:** French can-can, Polish mazurka, Caribbean calypso, Arabian dance
- **Jazz and blues:** ragtime, Dixieland/trad, Charleston, swing, big band, bebop, funk
- **Latin American:** rumba, bossa nova, samba, tango
- **Popular music:** rock 'n' roll, rhythm and blues, sixties, Motown, soul/ gospel, reggae, hip hop.

If my theme is from a specific period, do I have to stay there?
Not at all, as much of the thrill of arranging lies in the opportunity to push boundaries and break rules. Gareth Valentine, Musical Director and Dance Arranger for English National Ballet's *Strictly Gershwin*, explains his anachronistic approach:

'I didn't want to be chained wholly to the styles of the 20s and 30s ... and so I unapologetically dip into later musical trends.'

(Valentine, quoted in the ENB programme, 2011)

In order to be a successful and versatile arranger you will need to master – over a period of time – the basic characteristics of all of the above styles, plus any others you might like to consider. However, what follows is a shorthand guide to some of the above, so hopefully that will set you on your way to further investigation.

WORKING THROUGH POSSIBLE IDEAS

We now have our theme, have listened to examples of variations, and are reasonably confident with at least some of the categories listed above. Now it's time to experiment:

1. Make sure you know the original really well: sing it, play it, and ensure it is lodged in your head. This can be done at or away from the instrument: while driving, washing up, waiting to collect your child after school – a true arranger never stops working.
2. Experiment with various styles. Might the tune work as a march, or a samba? What about blues, or even reggae? Whatever your instrument, just play your tune over and over again, trying *anything you can think of*, and see what works. Could it be made to swing? Might it pass as a slow sarabande? At this stage don't be frightened to try anything, no matter how bizarre it may seem.

Witness author Marty Bell as he observes Broadway dance arranger Peter Howard in the early stages of creating the Act 1 finale of *Crazy for You* with choreographer Susan Stroman:

'...[Peter] Howard plays the tune [Gershwin's "I Got Rhythm"] as a tango, as a rag, a little honky-tonk, a little Hungarian. Then in the style of the 1812 Overture.'

(Bell, 1994)

Further questions to consider:

- Do some variations feel complete on their own, while others need to link to the next one?
- Of the dance structures you have chosen, which one might lend itself to an extended finale? A grand waltz perhaps, or a military march? Or maybe a *moto perpetuo* Irish reel as we hurtle towards the finish?
- What instruments might you use for each variation?

You will notice we have not referred to the major or minor contrast, or any key changes. This is not because they are unimportant – far from it – but they should really arise out of an instinctive need rather than being shoehorned into the piece. For example, a tango or sarabande will work very well in a minor key (arguably better than in the major), as would a rumba or blues. Similarly, a change of key may present itself as a necessity, possibly in a fast variation which would be over too quickly without extension and modulation.

Does the original theme need to appear in every variation?
Not necessarily. Once the melody and its associated harmony are firmly fixed in the listener's psyche you can depart from it. Whether it is well known or not should also be taken into account. However, most listeners will want to spot the theme wherever possible, so avoid complex **retrograde** (backwards) or **inversion** (upside-down) approaches if you can. *You* may be aware the tune is present, but nobody else will and that particular variation will end up as a damp squib.

MAPPING OUT

Once you have been through the experimental stage – although this should really be ongoing – it is time to produce a draft plan for your piece. Instead of thinking in separate variations, aim to link styles together as this will make more sense to the listener – thus you might decide to have a section of Latin-American dances and another which is jazz-based. An alternative approach is to group in terms of tempo – a sarabande, followed by a slow blues and gentle bossa nova, or a fast $\frac{6}{8}$ march leading into an Irish gigue.

You could then end up with: theme: march: gavotte; ragtime; swing; rock 'n' roll; tango; samba; $^6_8$ march; Irish gigue (extended finale).

Some variations will run through from one to another, others will work as single entities. It is also a good idea to have a halt in the middle to allow a restart. The obvious place in the above example might be after the rock 'n' roll section and before the tango (which is a very different genre, and may well be in a minor key).

The map above is flexible and open to discussion. You won't really find out whether it works until you try it with real instrumentalists, at which point things will become much clearer. Any opportunity to try your music on a regular basis with your ensemble should be grabbed with gusto, and never taken for granted – many arrangers will not be so lucky. It may be embarrassing in the early stages as what your members play bears little resemblance to what you had hoped to hear, but you must persevere. It is all part of an essential, unavoidable learning curve. As André Previn reminds us:

'No master at a conservatory, no matter how revered, can teach as much by verbal criticism as can a cold and analytical hearing of one's own music being played.'

(Previn, 1993)

ORCHESTRATION AND INSTRUMENTATION

This book cannot tell you exactly how to use the instruments at your disposal, as there is no way of knowing what you have to work with. However, it is possible to make some suggestions as to what might be advisable. Thus, in general terms, you will need:

- **High range:** flute/recorder, clarinet, violin, trumpet
- **Middle range:** horn, alto saxophone, viola, second/third clarinet
- **Bass line:** cello/bass, baritone/tenor saxophone, trombone/tuba
- **Percussion:** both tuned and untuned if possible (two to three players)
- **Piano/keyboard:** not essential, but can be very useful, both as an entity in itself and for filling in holes. A multi-sound keyboard can also be very effective at evoking styles – bluesy Hammond organ perhaps, French accordion or even Baroque harpsichord.

How many separate lines should I write?
In general, the fewer the better, as the textures will be much cleaner and the lines will be heard. Aim for a melody, accompaniment and bass line, augmented by percussion. You may also desire a countermelody or descant at times for stylistic reasons (such as the characteristic flute/piccolo descants in

Sousa marches), but, as a rule, avoid clutter and thick harmonies unless you are very confident, as too many lines can spoil an otherwise decent idea.

Doubling

Doubling lines is a good thing, especially with amateurs, as it reinforces each part and gives everyone confidence that they are not alone. It is also a good idea musically as it strengthens the line. Probably the most effective way of increasing the volume of an individual musical line is to add another instrument doing exactly the same. Octave doubling can also be effective, and certainly increases the impact of the part, whether it is the tune or a new countermelody.

Cueing

Look to write as many cues in the parts as possible, as they serve several purposes:

- **The standard cue** aids tricky entries, as the player can see what comes beforehand.
- **The doubling cue** enables another instrument to assist the original one if so desired, and depending on numbers on the day. Thus a trombone line might be cued in the tenor saxophone part, leaving the conductor with the option of one, the other or even both playing.
- **The colour cue** is perhaps the most useful at amateur level, as it allows the arranger to try different sounds and timbres to see which might work best in practice. An example might be the same melody appearing in the violin, flute and oboe part. In reality only one instrument will end up playing it, but you are not entirely sure which yet until you and/or the conductor have heard it. Having the cue there can also be useful for repeated sections, where the melody might be switched to another instrument the second time round.

Cues and optional lines – written as smaller notes – are a major asset to the beginner arranger, as they allow you to fix things during the rehearsal, with the minimum of fuss. Once decided upon, the parts can be marked accordingly and there is no need for any rewriting or reprinting. Even better, should the flautist be unavailable for a certain rehearsal or even the concert, there is no panic because the violinist has the part, has learned the line, and can step in at short notice.

The choice of key: why it matters

This is so much more important than it might first appear, and it is not a decision to be taken quickly. In a mixed instrumental ensemble, the issue is this:

Wind and brass players like *flat* keys: F, B♭, E♭, A♭, whereas string players, including guitarists, like *sharp* keys: G, D, A.

This presents the arranger with a problem, especially with young or inexperienced players. As a starting point, it is wise to go with the majority. Thus if your ensemble is predominantly string-based, go with the sharp keys; if it is mostly wind and brass, opt for the flat keys.

It also depends on which instrumentation you wish to feature in a particular variation. A Baroque string gavotte will not include clarinets or saxophones, so a sharp key can be chosen to suit the strings. However, the opposite will be true of a swing version, in which case the flat key choice is best.

The main thing to remember is not what key you are writing but what key the player will end up reading:

- In concert pitch: all strings, flutes, oboes, bassoons, trombones
- In B♭ (written a tone higher): clarinets, trumpets, tenor saxophones
- In E♭ (written a sixth higher): alto and baritone saxophones, tubas.

Thus, if the chosen concert key is F major, the B♭ instruments are reading in G major and the E♭ instruments are in D major – no problem. However, should the chosen concert key be G major, the results are very different: B♭ instruments find themselves with three sharps to negotiate, not to mention the E♭ players and their four sharps.

Key signatures and modulation

Starting keys are all very well, but the real problem comes with key changes. Consider the following: a starting key of B♭ major: B♭ instruments in C major, E♭ instruments in G major – fine to begin with.

Now let's think about the final chorus of a pop song, and the audience-pleasing, up-the-semitone modulation. The listeners may be happy, but spare a thought for the players, whose lives suddenly become very difficult indeed.

The new concert key is now B major (5 sharps): B♭ instruments are now in C♯ major, and E♭ instruments in G♯ major. This is not going to work at all.

A much better solution is to modulate up the *tone*, resulting in the keys of C, D and A respectively, or opt for the more conventional changes to the dominant (F major) or the subdominant (E♭ major).

Key changes, especially in lengthy pieces, can take on a life of their own and you may find yourself arriving in some unexpected places with far too many sharps or flats. If this happens, take a moment, work backwards, and see whether there is a way of rectifying the problem, ideally by opting for a different key earlier on in the process.

If in doubt, always remember composer and teacher William Russo's salutary warning, which applies just as much to choices of key as it does to high notes and rapid fingering:

'Technically, it is always better to err on the side of simplicity than on the side of complexity. Music which is beneath the technical levels of the musicians will be played well. Music that is the slightest bit too hard may not be played at all.'

(Russo, 1973)

DAISY BELL VARIATIONS

We are now ready to write some actual variations on our tune. The rest of this chapter outlines examples of possible starts based on the six stylistic models discussed earlier. A reduced annotated score has been provided as an example of a military march, and further examples for each model along with audio recordings are available on the book's companion website.

First, a reminder of the six stylistic models that can be used for the variations:

1. Military
2. Formal/classical
3. Jazz and blues
4. Latin-American
5. Nationalistic
6. Popular music.

What follows is one example of each of the above models, categorised under the following elements:

- **Melody** – what alterations need to be made to the original?
- **Harmony** – what chords and intervals are appropriate to the style?
- **Introduction** – does it need one or not?
- **Mood/atmosphere** – what are we trying to do here?
- **Instrumentation** – which instruments establish the style?
- **Piano/keyboard** – what sounds should be used, and why?
- **Untuned percussion** – what is needed, and why?
- **Tuned percussion** – anything that might add colour to melodies/ countermelodies.

- **Original model** – the classic traditional version.
- **Commercial/pastiche model** – the Hollywood/Broadway equivalent.

There will also be a suggested level of difficulty for the players (easy/medium/difficult).

1. Military

Example A: $\frac{4}{4}$ March

- Melody: additional dotted rhythms
- Harmony: straight primary harmony
- Introduction: yes, with snare drum prominent
- Mood/atmosphere: establish military feel
- Instrumentation: brass and percussion, some wind, no strings
- Piano/keyboard: not needed if there is a tuba/trombone, otherwise basic piano pattern
- Untuned percussion: kit – snare, bass, cymbals
- Tuned percussion: glockenspiel (aka bells) for Sousa feel
- Original model: Sousa's 'Stars and Stripes for Ever'
- Commercial/pastiche model: Elmer Bernstein's theme for *The Great Escape*, Julian Nott's *Wallace and Gromit*
- Difficulty level: medium, provided you have a decent snare drummer.

2. Formal/classical style

An example of a gavotte can be found on the book's companion website.

Example B: Viennese Waltz

Note: although the original theme is already in 3 time, it will still need some adapting to make it feel truly waltz-like.

- Melody: more broken up, with second beat lift
- Harmony: straight primary harmony
- Introduction: yes, but simple
- Mood/atmosphere: ballroom
- Instrumentation: light wind and strings
- Piano/keyboard: yes, but mostly for harp effects
- Untuned percussion: light triangle
- Original model: waltzes of Johann Strauss and Franz Lehar
- Commercial/pastiche model: Leowe's waltz from *My Fair Lady*, Rodgers' 'Carousel Waltz'
- Difficulty level: medium, although achieving the requisite lightness may be a challenge.

3. Jazz styles

Explanations, examples and recordings of Charleston and Big Band styles can be found on the book's companion website.

Example C: Ragtime

- Melody: syncopated, with chromatic colouring
- Harmony: mostly simple, with some secondary harmony
- Introduction: yes, stylistic, unison
- Mood/atmosphere: light, and not hurried
- Instrumentation: light woodwind, muted brass, strings
- Piano/keyboard: the original ragtime instrument, so prominent
- Untuned percussion: simple kit, plus temple block colour
- Tuned percussion: xylophone
- Original model: Scott Joplin: 'The Entertainer', 'Maple Leaf Rag'
- Commercial/pastiche model: Marvin Hamlisch's score for *The Sting*
- Difficulty level: medium, but must be stylish.

4. Latin-American styles

An example of a Brazilian samba can be found on the book's companion website.

Example D: Tango – in D minor (the relative minor, that is the same key signature)

- Melody: similar to original, but march-like

- Harmony: mostly primary, but occasional flattened 7th suggests modal feel
- Introduction: unison figures, with imitation
- Mood/atmosphere: strict, passionate
- Instrumentation: full wind and brass, with strings countermelody
- Piano/keyboard: yes, simple patterns, possibility of accordion sound
- Untuned percussion: snare/bass drum, with colour castanets
- Tuned percussion: xylophone picks out melodic motifs
- Original model: Astor Piazzolla tangos
- Commercial/pastiche model: Adler and Ross's 'Hernando's Hideaway' (*The Pajama Game*)
- Difficulty level: medium, although the string parts are challenging.

5. Nationalistic styles

An example of a French can-can is available on the book's companion website.

Example E: Arabian – in D minor (the relative minor, that is same key signature)

- Melody: based on original, but exploiting augmented 2nd interval at top of harmonic minor scale
- Harmony: mostly primary, with plenty of open 5ths for bass drone
- Introduction: pulsing bass, plus Arabian scale
- Mood/atmosphere: hot and hazy
- Instrumentation: oboe is the key instrument here, plus strings – thin texture
- Piano/keyboard: drone, plus spread chords
- Untuned percussion: mostly for colour – tambourine, cymbal, triangle
- Original model: Tchaikovsky's Arabian Dance from *The Nutcracker*
- Commercial/pastiche model: Wright and Forrest's 'Sands of Time' (from *Kismet*)
- Difficulty level: easy, assuming a strong oboe player.

6. Popular music style

Example F: 1960s' Bossa Nova in C major (the dominant)

- Melody: light and very syncopated
- Harmony: mostly primary, with some chromaticism
- Introduction: percussion, bass, pizzicato strings
- Mood/atmosphere: fun/light-hearted
- Instrumentation: flute melody (plus trombone), muted trumpets, low saxes
- Piano/keyboard: yes, to provide countermelody

- Untuned percussion: kit, tambourine, bongos, cabasa (some of which could be played by band members)
- Tuned percussion: xylophone doubles a mixture of countermelody and tune
- Original model: Quincy Jones' 'Soul Bossa Nova' (as used in *Austin Powers*)
- Commercial/pastiche model: 'Rich Man's Frug' (from *Sweet Charity*)
- Difficulty level: medium, with quite a few interlocking lines.

The above examples, plus those available on the website – are just some possible approaches to arranging this melody, and there are plenty more. Maybe you have already thought of another? As an alternative, you might take one of the resulting variations above and develop it into a full-length piece. Feel free to do so or, better still, take a different theme, follow the steps above, and see what you can come up with. Start to explore possibilities.

A complete instrumental arrangement of the 'Daisy Bell' variations is available to download on the book's companion website.

As you become more experienced, and willing to be a little braver, you will begin to see the great attraction of musical arranging. Not only will it make your group sound good, but there will be something much more for you as an individual, a need to express yourself. Once you catch the arranging bug there is no cure, and almost every tune you hear – new or old – will instantly start transforming itself in your head.

Let us leave the final words to the musicians themselves, firstly to Don Sebesky, on the importance of continual growth, and finally to Ian Carr, writing in his autobiography of Miles Davis about the collaboration between Davis and arranger Gil Evans on the *Porgy and Bess* suite:

Practical

'Listen, evaluate, analyse, study … Learn to trust the judgment of your ear instead of your eye. Music does not exist on paper.'

(Sebesky, 1994)

Inspirational

'They [Davis and Evans] do more than justice to Gershwin's great opera, transforming it, deepening it, and uncovering roots of which even Gershwin was probably unaware.'

(Carr, 1999)

GENERAL

Bell, M. (1994) *Backstage on Broadway*. Nick Hern Books.

Carr, I. (1999) *Miles Davis: The Definitive Biography*. Harper Collins.

Hindley, G. (ed) (1982) *The Larousse Encyclopedia of Music*. Hamlyn.

Previn, A. (1993) *No Minor Chords: My Days in Hollywood*. Bantam, London.

Shaw, S. in *Music Teacher*. Rhinegold Publishing.

Sondheim, S. (2011) *Look, I Made a Hat*, Virgin Books. New York.

Stanley, S. (ed) (1988) *The Grove Concise Dictionary Of Music*. Macmillan.

Stein Crease, S. (2002) *Gil Evans: Out of the Cool*. A Capella.

Valentine, G. (2011) Programme for 'Strictly Gershwin'. English National
    Ballet.

Younghusband, J. (1991) *Orchestra!* Chatto and Windus.

ARRANGING

Erickson, F. (1983) *Arranging for the Concert Band*. Alfred, California.

Mancini, H. (1962) *Sounds and Scores*. Northridge, USA.

Runswick, D. (1992) *Rock, Jazz and Pop Arranging*. Faber, London.

Russo, W. (1973) *Composing for the Jazz Orchestra*. University of Chicago
    Press.

Sebesky, D. (1994) *The Contemporary Arranger*. Alfred, California.

Wright, R. (1983) *Inside the Score*. Kendor.

MEDIA

Sir Colin Davis, quoted as advice by Charles Hazelwood in his lecture
    Trusting the Ensemble (www.ted.com).

Donald Runnicles, quoted in *Conducting Masterclasses* with the BBC
    Scottish SO (2010).

Peter Stark, conducting mentor, quoted on the BBC's *Maestro* website
    (www.bbc.co.uk/musictv/maestro)

Bill Bailey's Remarkable Guide to the Orchestra (DVD Universal 2009)

Michael Buble: quoted from *Entertainment Weekly* (www.ew.com)

Richard Niles' History of Pop Arranging, documentary BBC 2003

VOCAL WARM-UPS

The following books are worth reading for guidance on vocal warm-ups:

Brewer, M. (2002) *Warm Ups.* Faber Music
Crocker, E. (1989) *Warm Ups and Work Outs for the Developing Choir.*
    Hal Leonard
Heizmann, K. (2004) *Vocal Warm Ups: 200 exercises for choral and solo*
    singers. Schott Music

AUTHOR'S NOTE

Many thanks to the following:

Tim Venvell for the loan of his André Previn book
James Manwaring for drawing my attention to the Schott choral warm-up book
Elen Monwayne for her advice on singing outside
Richard Whennell for his outstanding vocal arranging for Glee Club UK
Chris Byatt for his ongoing software assistance

This glossary has been deliberately simplified for the context of this book, and is not intended to be definitive. More in-depth definitions for each term may be found in resources such as the Rhinegold Dictionary of Music in Sound.

Augmentation: the lengthening of note values.

Cadence: a progression of two or three chords to end a musical phrase.

Chord sequence: a series of chords producing a pattern, for instance 12 bar blues.

Contrary motion: simultaneous musical lines moving in opposite directions.

Countermelody: a new melodic line which is designed to fit a pre-existing tune.

Descant: a melodic line above the basic tune, such as in a hymn.

Diminished harmony: chords based on diminished intervals, for instance diminished 7th, flattened 5th.

Dissonance: clashing notes/harmonies, often using the intervals of 2nds/7ths.

Dominant: the fifth note of the scale.

Dominant 7th: the triad of the fifth chord of the scale, with an additional minor third on top, frequently used for modulation at a cadence.

Extension chord: intervals built on top of the basic triad, such as 7ths, 9ths, 11ths and 13ths, designed to enrich the harmony.

False relation: the simultaneous and/or adjacent appearance, in different parts/lines, of a note in its natural version and its chromatically altered equivalent.

Harmonic rhythm: the rate at which the chords change, for instance one chord per bar. The harmonic rhythm often increases at the approach to cadence.

Harmonic structure: see **Chord sequence**.

Head arrangement: a simple arrangement which is not written down but is created by the performers during the rehearsal and then memorised.

Internal modulation: this is where the given melody includes a key change in its original chord sequence.

Inversion: any chord where the bass note is not the root, for instance C major with an E at the bottom instead of C.

Inverted pedal: a pedal note, sustained or repeated, at the top of the texture (rather than in the bass).

Modal: music which is not in a major or minor key but is instead based on one of the 'church modes' (such as Dorian, Aeolian, Mixolydian). These will usually be identified by the flattened 7th interval in the melodic line.

Modulation: the process of changing key.

Motif: a short segment (rhythmic or melodic) of a longer phrase, from which much of the ensuing music is derived.

Ostinato: a repeating idea, similar to a riff in popular music.

Parallel: two or more parts moving in the same direction (as opposed to **Contrary motion**), and keeping the same interval apart. Parallel 3rds and 6ths are the standard way of producing the **thickened line**.

Passing note: a note that does not fit with the prevailing harmony, for instance F against a C major triad.

Pastiche: a conscious (and acknowledged) attempt to compose/arrange in the style of a well-known composer.

Pedal note: a sustained or repeated note in the bass, over which the harmony changes.

Primary harmony: based on the chords of I, IV or V, for instance chords C, F or G in C major.

Resolution: a transition from a dissonant note to a consonant note.

Retrograde: the motif or theme is written/played backwards.

Root position: the key note of the chord is at the bottom, for instance G at the bottom of a G major chord (compare with 'Inversion' above).

Second inversion: a chord with the 5th at the bottom, for instance A at the bottom of a D major chord.

Secondary harmony: based on the chords of II and VI, for instance the chords of G minor and D minor in the key of F major.

Strophic: a song structure which uses the same music for each verse (although there may be some small adaptations to enable the words to fit).

Subdominant: the fourth note of the scale.

Submediant: the sixth note of the scale.

Substitution: replacing a primary chord with a secondary/extended chord to produce harmonic variety, perhaps when harmonising the same melody twice, for instance in G major, chord I (G) may be replaced by chord VI (E minor) if the melody fits.

Supertonic: the second note of the scale.

Suspension: the same held/repeated note is at first consonant, then dissonant, then consonant again as the harmonies change underneath it.

Thickened line: when a single melodic line is harmonised using parallel intervals, such as 3rds, 6ths or 8ves.

Transposing instruments: instruments that are not 'in concert', for instance a B♭ trumpet will need to be written a tone higher to produce the same note as an oboe.

Transposition: putting the music into a different key, usually via modulation (see above).

Unison: a specific texture in which the instruments/singers are playing/singing exactly the same line at the same time.